LONGM

KEYSTONE

B

Assessment

PEARSON
Longman

LONGMAN
KEYSTONE **B**

Keystone B Assessment

Pearson Education, 10 Bank Street, White Plains, NY 10606

Staff credits: The people who made up the *Longman Keystone* team, representing editorial, production, design, manufacturing, and marketing, are John Ade, Rhea Banker, Liz Barker, Danielle Belfiore, Don Bensey, Virginia Bernard, Kenna Bourke, Anne Boynton-Trigg, Johnnie Farmer, Maryann Finocchi, Patrice Fraccio, Geraldine Geniusas, Charles Green, Henry Hild, David L. Jones, Lucille M. Kennedy, Ed Lamprich, Emily Lippincott, Tara Maceyak, Maria Pia Marrella, Linda Moser, Laurie Neaman, Sherri Pemberton, Liza Pleva, Joan Poole, Edie Pullman, Monica Rodriguez, Tania Saiz-Sousa, Chris Siley, Lynn Sobotta, Heather St. Clair, Jennifer Stem, Siobhan Sullivan, Jane Townsend, Heather Vomero, Marian Wassner, Lauren Weidenman, Matthew Williams, and Adina Zoltan.

Cover Image: background, John Foxx/Getty Images; inset, Stockbyte/Getty Images
Text composition: TSI Graphics
Text font: 11 pt ITC Stone Sans Std

ISBN-13: 978-0-13-233977-3
ISBN-10: 0-13-233977-3

PEARSON LONGMAN ON THE **WEB**

Pearsonlongman.com offers online resources for teachers and students. Access our Companion Websites, our online catalog, and our local offices around the world.

Visit us at **pearsonlongman.com**.

Printed in the United States of America
2 3 4 5 6 7 8 9 10 11—CRS—13 12 11 10 09 08

CONTENTS

INTRODUCTION

The *Keystone Assessment* book provides a variety of tests to help you assess students' understanding of the reading selections and the skills taught in the *Keystone* program. The Assessment book was also designed to help students become better test takers. Key test preparation strategies help students become better test takers, by providing them with opportunities to answer questions similar to those found on many standardized tests.

Description of Tests

Diagnostic Pretest

The Diagnostic Pretest is based on a readiness for skills taught in this level of *Keystone*. It contains two listening passages: one narrative and one informative. It also includes two reading passages: one narrative and one functional. Students answer multiple-choice questions about these passages and about the vocabulary, morphology, phonics, spelling, and grammar skills taught in the Student Book. The test includes a writing prompt based on a type of writing taught in the Student Book, as well as an oral reading fluency check. This test provides teachers with a tool for determining which skills individual students or groups of students may need to improve.

Midterm Test

The Midterm Test measures students' proficiency with skills taught in Units 1–3. It contains two listening passages: one narrative and one informative. It also includes two reading passages: one narrative and one functional. Students answer multiple-choice questions about these passages and about the vocabulary, morphology, phonics, spelling, and grammar skills taught in the Student Book. The test includes a writing prompt based on a type of writing taught in the Student Book, as well as an oral fluency check.

Posttest

The Posttest measures students' proficiency with skills taught in this level of *Keystone*. It contains two listening passages: one narrative and one informative. It also includes two reading passages: one narrative and one functional. Students answer multiple-choice questions about these passages and about the vocabulary, morphology, phonics, spelling, and grammar skills taught in the Student Book. The test includes a writing prompt based on a type of writing taught in the Student Book, as well as an oral fluency check.

Reading Tests

There are four Reading Tests for each unit of the Student Book, twenty-four Reading Tests in all. Each test is based on the skills and text selections in the Reading. Students answer multiple-choice questions about the selections, the literary or key vocabulary, the academic words, word study, reading strategies, and grammar, usage, and mechanics presented in the Student Book.

Unit Tests

There is one Unit Test for each unit of the Student Book, six Unit Tests in all. Each test is based on the skills and text selections from all four Reading sections of a unit. It includes a listening passage, either narrative or informative, that is linked to the unit theme. Students answer multiple-choice questions about the listening passage and the Student Book text selections. They also answer questions about literary and key vocabulary, academic words, word study, reading strategies, and grammar, usage, and mechanics skills. Each test includes a writing prompt based on the Big Question, as well as an oral reading fluency check.

Test Preparation Pages

At the end of this Assessment Package is a section with test preparation strategies. This section raises students' awareness of different kinds of test items and provides them with strategies to use. Sample test questions and a writing prompt are provided, so students can practice applying each strategy.

ADMINISTERING THE TESTS

Planning and Scheduling Tests

Diagnostic Pretest: Administer the Diagnostic Pretest at the beginning of the year to assess students' readiness for the skills that will be taught in *Keystone*.

Midterm Test: Administer the Midterm Test after students have finished Unit 3 to assess students' progress since taking the Diagnostic Pretest.

Posttest: Administer the Posttest at the end of the year to assess students' progress since beginning the course.

Reading Tests: Administer each Reading Test after finishing the related part in the Student Book.

Unit Tests: Administer each Unit Test after finishing the related unit in the Student Book. The Unit Tests cover the same skills as the Reading Tests, but each test has different questions or items. Therefore, you could choose to administer the Unit Test in place of the Reading Tests or in addition to the Reading Tests.

Test Preparation Pages: The Test Preparation pages can be used at any time during the year prior to taking a test.

The chart below gives an overview of the tests in this Assessment book. Use the chart to help you plan and schedule the tests.

Test	Test Sections	Total Items
Diagnostic Pretest, Midterm Test, Posttest	Listening and Reading Comprehension Vocabulary Word Study Grammar Writing Oral Reading Fluency	50 multiple-choice items writing prompt oral reading fluency check
Reading Test	Key or Literary Words Academic Words Word Study Reading Grammar	30 multiple-choice items
Unit Test	Listening and Reading Comprehension Vocabulary Word Study Grammar Writing Oral Reading Fluency	55 multiple-choice items writing prompt oral reading fluency check

Directions for Administering the Tests

The following directions are general instructions that can be used for all tests. Instructions can be modified, based on how you choose to administer each test.

Before You Administer a Test

Review the test to familiarize yourself with its contents. Make copies of the test for students and yourself. The Diagnostic Pretest, the Midterm Test, the Posttest, and the Unit Tests each have listening passages that you can read aloud or you can use the program's audio program. If you choose to read a passage aloud, preview it before you administer the test, and have the appropriate passage(s) on hand during the listening section of the test. Listening passages begin on page vii of this Assessment book. Audio for the Listening passages can be found at www.LongmanKeystone.com.

When You Are Ready to Administer a Test

Make sure students' desks are cleared and that they have pens or pencils for marking their tests. The Diagnostic Pretest, the Midterm Test, the Posttest, and the Unit Tests each have a writing prompt with lines for students' responses. You may wish to provide students with extra lined paper for planning or for additional space to write their responses. Distribute copies of the test to students, and have students write their names on their tests. Describe the contents of the test or the section of the test that you are administering. Point out important features of the test, such as the directions, questions and items, answer choices, writing prompt, and Go On or Stop symbols. Make sure students understand that they are to mark their answers by circling only one letter for each multiple-choice question, and that they should write their response to a writing prompt on the lines below the prompt. Answer any questions that students may have, and then start the test. If you set a time limit for the test, tell students how much time they have for the test session and write the ending time on the board. Give students a five-minute warning before you end the test session.

The oral reading fluency section of the Diagnostic Pretest, Midterm, Posttest, and Unit Tests will need to be administered individually to each student. You may choose to administer this section as students are completing the writing prompt.

After the Test

Directions for scoring the tests are on page xi. Use the Answer Key and Tested Skills Charts that begin on page xxiii to score each test. Use the Writing Scoring Rubric on page xii to assess responses to writing prompts. Use the Oral Reading Fluency Score Sheets to assess oral reading fluency. The Answer Key and Tested Skills Charts can also help you determine students' areas of strength and diagnose problem areas.

LISTENING PASSAGES

When conducting the Listening Comprehension portion of the Diagnostic Pretest, Midterm, Posttest, or Unit Test, you may read the appropriate listening passage aloud or have students listen to the passage on the audio program. Read or play each passage twice, and then pause for students to complete the questions. Have students continue on to the next section of the test when they have finished answering.

Diagnostic Pretest:
Passage 1: Benny's Birthday Blues

Benny invited many classmates to his birthday party. By 7:00 p.m., everyone had arrived.

As they stood in the living room, Benny said, "I've made a list of things we are going to do." Out of his pocket, Benny pulled a list as long as his arm. "First, you can watch me cut my birthday cake." The chocolate cake looked delicious.

"I can't wait to try a piece," Rosa said, reaching for a plate.

"We're not going to eat until after I open my presents," Benny said. Everyone sat quietly as Benny opened each present. If Benny liked a present, then he said, "Thank you." If he didn't like a present, then he didn't say anything.

After a little while, Hafez said, "I have to go home now."

"But it is still early," Benny said, "and it's Friday."

One by one everyone left. Benny wondered what went wrong. He had planned everything so carefully.

Passage 2: A Great Idea

The book you are reading now, like nearly all books, was printed at a printing press. It is easy to read because it was printed on clean, white paper with black ink.

Johannes Gutenberg, a German goldsmith, invented the printing press in the mid-1400s'. Ink was rolled over wooden letters and then pressed onto a sheet of paper. Gutenberg's invention made printing faster, easier, and less expensive. Furthermore, his invention changed more than the world of printing.

The printing press allowed scientists and other scholars to share information and communicate their discoveries. The invention of the printing press also gave more people the chance to learn to read and to write.

Today's printing presses are even faster, able to produce millions of copies in just one day. It all started with a great idea several centuries ago.

Midterm Test:
Passage 1: Javier and Max

Javier and Max do everything together. They splash in the river, climb over logs, and find spiders and other insects. Javier sometimes throws a stick and Max catches it in mid-air. However, at night, Max sleeps outside and Javier sleeps in his bedroom.

"Max is a dog and dogs belong outside," Javier's mother always says.

One night, as Javier was just finishing his homework, his mother came into his room to say good night. Suddenly, they heard a scratching at the window. Javier ran to the window and looked out. It was Max!

"You see, mom? Max wants to stay with me!"

His mother laughed. "It does look that way, doesn't it?"

"Can I let him sleep in my room?"

"Well . . . okay."

Javier leaped up from his desk and ran to the front door. "Come on in, Max. We will be roommates from now on."

Passage 2: California's Redwoods

What is the highest you have ever ridden in an elevator? Ten floors? Twenty? If you rode an elevator up thirty floors, you would be up as high as some of the tallest trees in the world—the California redwoods. Imagine ten grown men standing side-by-side. This is how wide a redwood's trunk is!

Heavy rainfall, fog and cool air from the ocean help keep the forest wet all year. This keeps the huge trees healthy and enables them to grow taller every day. In fact, when you look up, you cannot see the top of a redwood. If you could fly like a bird over the treetops, you would discover a whole new world. Unique plants and animals live hundreds of feet up in the redwoods' branches.

Many people like to visit big cities to gaze up at tall skyscrapers. California's redwood forest is a magical place where you can see nature's skyscrapers.

Posttest:

Passage 1: A Tossed Salad of Words

Dear Habib,

I read an interesting article about Native Americans yesterday. I never knew that many names of U.S. cities and states come from Native American words! For example, Ohio is an Iroquois word that means "fine river" and Kansas is a Sioux word that means "south wind people."

This made me curious about other words, so I looked up some words in the dictionary. I discovered something as valuable as gold! After the meaning of each word, it tells the origin, or what language the word comes from. I discovered that many words come from Greek and Latin. I also found some words that come from French, Spanish, and Arabic. Since I'm from a foreign country myself, I'm excited to learn that English is a tossed salad of words from around the world.

I think I will go eat a *tomato* now (that's a Nahuatl word from Mexico)!

Your friend,

Rita

Passage 2: Lighting up the Dark

Have you ever tried walking in your house at night? It is dark and you bump your knee or stub your toe. Perhaps you've even wished that you had a light built right into your finger or your forehead.

Some creatures that live in dark places do have built-in lights. For example, fish that live in the deep parts of the ocean have tiny organs on their bodies that produce light. Usually the light is a blue-green color because it travels best in water. Lanternfish use their lights to attract small fish that they eat or to signal other lanternfish during mating. Some sea creatures use light to find their way—kind of like how we use a flashlight.

Deep sea creatures are not the only animals with the ability to produce light, however. Have you ever looked out your window at night and seen little lights flashing in the air? Fireflies flash their lights to attract other fireflies, creating a fantastic "fireworks" display even when it's not the 4th of July!

Unit 1 Test
Passage: All About Parrots

Parrots are very smart. They like to repeat what they hear around them. Suppose a parrot hears your mother say, "Do your homework." The next day, you might hear the parrot say, "Do your homework!"

Parrots can do more than just repeat words. They can think, too. A scientist taught a parrot to describe and count objects. Another parrot has learned one thousand words!

Parrots don't just say words; they can imitate sounds, too. A parrot that lives with a noisy dog might learn how to bark. If you are thinking about getting a pet, you should consider getting a parrot!

Unit 2 Test
Passage: A Rainbow without Rain

My neighbor Mrs. Bloom loves flowers. Her yard was a rainbow of colorful flowers until the rain stopped. Well, the rain didn't stop completely. It just wasn't enough to keep Mrs. Bloom's flowers happy. They drooped and turned brown. One morning, I was surprised to see Mrs. Bloom digging them up.

I walked over to her yard. "Mrs. Bloom, what are you doing with your flowers?"

"Well, Thomas, we just don't get much rain anymore, so I've decided to dig them up."

I couldn't imagine Mrs. Bloom having a yard without flowers. "Won't you miss having a pretty yard?" I asked.

"Oh, I will still have a pretty yard. Come on, I'll show you something." We entered a small building. Strange flowers I'd never seen before bloomed in pots. "These flowers don't need much water, so I'm going to plant them instead."

Now, even without rain, Mrs. Bloom's yard looks like a rainbow again.

Unit 3 Test
Passage: A W-i-n-n-e-r!

Before June 2007, not many people had heard of Evan O'Dorney. Then Evan won the Scripps National Spelling Bee. The contest is held every year in Washington, D.C. Evan competed with other spellers for many hours. When a student spells a word incorrectly, the student is out of the contest.

After thirteen long rounds, Evan won. "Serrefine" was the word he spelled correctly to win the spelling bee. A *serrefine* is a medical instrument used by doctors. Evan says that memorizing words is easy, but that spelling is not his favorite thing to do. His favorite subject is math because he likes the "way the numbers fit together" when he solves math problems. He also likes to write music because he can "let out ideas by composing notes." Evan was awarded a trophy, $35,000, and a $5,000 scholarship! I bet that makes you want to study the words in your d-i-c-t-i-o-n-a-r-y!

Unit 4 Test
Passage: Bored Bailey

Bailey flops on his bed. There's nothing to do. He lifts his head and looks around. Surely, there must be something to do. Bailey goes to the kitchen. He looks up at the table. There is something hanging over the edge—what is it? He jumps and grabs it. It smells delicious! He eats it in a few bites. Later, as he's ripping up some newspaper, the door opens. His friend, Marcus, frowns. "Bailey! What did you do?" Bailey feels guilty and folds his ears down in shame. Marcus kneels down in front of him. "I know you're bored. I wouldn't like to stay home all day either." The next day, Marcus takes Bailey to the beach where there are other dogs—some are digging in sand, some are chasing balls. A few are swimming. There is so much to do! At the end of the day, Bailey is tired, but happy. He hopes Marcus will bring him to play again tomorrow.

Unit 5 Test
Passage: Space, the Final Frontier

Most of us think that space is, well, just empty space. Not so! Space is actually filled with rocks, the most massive ones called "asteroids." Composed of rock and iron, asteroids are different from those other space rocks, comets, which are mostly rock and ice. Also, asteroids don't have tails like comets. Since asteroids are very similar to planets and moons in many ways, scientists often call asteroids "minor planets."

Like planets, some asteroids have been named and have moons. For example, when the Galileo flew past asteroid Ida in 1993, scientists discovered it had a moon.

Most asteroids orbit the sun between Mars and Jupiter. Not surprisingly, scientists have named this region the "asteroid belt." Even though there are millions of asteroids in the asteroid belt alone, asteroids are difficult to see because they don't stand out against the blackness of outer space.

Listening Passages

Unit 6 Test
Passage: Oh, Brother!

"What is pink and happy and lives on your face?" my little brother Gerry asked when I came home from school. Gerry likes to tell riddles, little puzzles that make you have to use your brain.

Before I could answer, he shouted, "A smile!"

I walked into the kitchen to get an after-school snack. Gerry followed me, "What's hot and yellow and looks like a ball?"

I poured a glass of milk. "The sun," I said. Are all little brothers so bothersome? "What's…" Gerry started to say.

"No more riddles!" I exclaimed under my breath.

Gerry's smile turned into a frown.

"Okay, you can tell me one more," I said, "but then I have to do my homework." "What's smart and cool and bigger than me?"

I shrugged. "I don't know."

"You are!" Gerry shouted.

I smiled. "You're smart and cool, too, little brother. And that isn't a riddle."

Use the Answer Key and Tested Skills Charts that begin on page xxiii of this Assessment book, the Writing Scoring Rubric on page xii, and the Oral Reading Fluency Score Sheet within each test to help you score students' tests. To score a test, follow these steps:

1. Find the appropriate Answer Key and Tested Skills Chart for the test to be scored. Make a copy of this chart for each student. Write the student's name at the top of the chart.

2. Check the student's answer for each multiple-choice item against the correct answer listed on the chart. Circle the student's score for each multiple-choice item on the chart. Award 1 point for each correct answer and 0 points for any incorrect answers.

3. The Diagnostic Pretest, the Midterm Test, the Posttest, and the Unit Tests each have a writing prompt and an oral fluency check in addition to multiple-choice questions. Use the Writing Scoring Rubric on page xii of this Assessment book to assess the student's response to the prompt. Award the student a score from 0 to 10 points for the response, and circle that score on the chart. For the oral reading fluency check, it is suggested that you time the student. You may wish to set a time limit of one minute and record how many words the student has read, or record the student's time after he or she has completed the entire passage. Using the page provided, you may mark the text in regards to hesitation or pauses, accuracy, expression, intonation, and self-correction. Then use the Oral Reading Fluency Score Sheet to award the student a score. A copy of the score sheet may be given to the student.

4. Use the formula below the chart to help you calculate a percent score for each test. Add the points circled to find the student's total score for the test and mark that total in the first blank in the formula. Then divide the total score by the total number of possible points that a student could earn on the test. Finally, multiply the quotient by 100 to get a percent score for the test.

Interpreting Test Results

A student's percent score on a test provides only one measurement of the student's progress and should be interpreted along with other assessments and observations. Students with consistently high scores may need more challenging assignments. Students with consistently low scores probably need a closer review of their progress and perhaps additional instruction and practice.

Use the student's completed Answer Key and Tested Skills Chart as a diagnostic tool. Each test item has been linked to a tested skill and to the relevant standard. Review the tested skills and assessed standards for the items the student answers correctly as well as for the items answered incorrectly. Look for patterns in the tested skills or assessed standards that indicate the student's strengths, as well as areas where the student may require additional instruction and practice. Use the following resources as needed to provide students with instruction, practice, or support.

- Student Book
- Teacher's Edition
- Audio CD
- Workbook
- Reader's Companion Workbook

- Student CD-ROM and e-book
- Teacher's Resource Book
- Video Program
- Transparencies

WRITING SCORING RUBRIC

Use the following rubric to help you assess students' responses to the writing prompts in the Diagnostic Pretest, the Midterm Test, the Posttest, and the Unit Tests. Each response should receive a score from 0 to 10 points, with 10 points being the highest score.

Score	Criteria
10	The composition as a whole is focused, well organized, and complete. It shows fresh insight into the writing task. Ideas flow in a logical order, and transitions are used effectively. The writing is marked by a sense of completeness and coherence. A main idea is fully developed, and support is specific and substantial. The writing voice is clear and lively. A mature command of the language is evident in the student's choice of words. Sentence structure is varied, and the writing is free of fragments. Virtually no errors in writing conventions appear.
8	The composition is focused on the task and complete, but the organization could be improved. Ideas flow logically, but the composition may also include some repetition or contain some ideas that are less developed than others. A main idea is well developed and supported with relevant detail. The student chooses precise words and has a clear voice. Sentence structure is varied, and the writing is free of fragments. Any errors in writing conventions are minor and do not impair the fluency of the writing.
6	The composition is focused on the task, but unrelated material sometimes intrudes. Occasionally, the writing shifts suddenly from idea to idea without a smooth transition, but the relationships between ideas remain clear. A clear organizational pattern is present, though lapses occur. The writing may also include irrelevant information, repetition, gaps in ideas, or lists of undeveloped ideas. A main idea is adequately supported, but development may be uneven. Sentence structure is free of fragments but usually lacks variation. The student demonstrates a limited command of writing conventions. Errors in spelling and punctuation may not obscure meaning but do weaken the overall fluency of the composition.
4	The composition is focused on the task, but unrelated material intrudes. Some organization is evident, but the writing lacks a logical progression of ideas. The composition shifts suddenly from idea to idea without a logical or smooth transition. Support for the main idea is present but is sometimes illogical. Sentence structure is free of fragments, but there is almost no sentence variety. The student's choice of words is sometimes inappropriate for the topic or audience, and the writing voice is unclear or inconsistent. The composition demonstrates some knowledge of writing conventions, with misspellings.
2	The composition has a weak connection to the task. It lacks focus or organization. The writing is fragmented, with no clear main idea. The writing voice does not convey the student's feelings or ideas. Sentence structure is unvaried, and serious errors appear. Poor choice of words and poor command of the language obscure meaning. Errors in writing conventions and spelling are frequent.
0	The composition is unrelated to the task or is simply a rewording of the prompt. It is copied from a published work, or it is illegible. The words in the response are not arranged in a meaningful way. There may be no response or an insufficient amount of writing to score.

Writing Scoring Rubric

Answer	Tested Skill	Score
Listening and Reading Comprehension		(Circle one.)
1. B	Listening/Answer Questions	0 1
2. B	Listening/Answer Questions	0 1
3. D	Listening/Character Motivation	0 1
4. B	Listening/Character Motivation	0 1
5. A	Listening/Comprehension	0 1
6. C	Listening/Answer Questions	0 1
7. B	Listening/Answer Questions	0 1
8. B	Listening/Comprehension	0 1
9. D	Character Motivation/ Identify Cause and Effect	0 1
10. B	Plot	0 1
11. B	Plot/Answer Questions	0 1
12. A	Plot/Answer Questions	0 1
13. C	Comprehension	0 1
14. A	Answer Questions	0 1
15. B	Answer Questions	0 1
16. C	Answer Questions	0 1
Vocabulary		
17. B	Literary Words	0 1
18. C	Literary Words	0 1
19. D	Literary Words	0 1
20. C	Literary Words	0 1
21. B	Literary Words	0 1
22. A	Literary Words	0 1
23. A	Literary Words	0 1
24. C	Key Words	0 1
25. C	Key Words	0 1
26. A	Key Words	0 1
27. B	Key Words	0 1
28. D	Key Words	0 1
29. C	Key Words	0 1
30. B	Academic Words	0 1
31. B	Academic Words	0 1
32. D	Academic Words	0 1
33. A	Academic Words	0 1

Answer	Tested Skill	Score
Word Study		(Circle one.)
34. A	Spelling	0 1
35. B	Spelling	0 1
36. A	Spelling	0 1
37. D	Prefixes	0 1
38. B	Spelling	0 1
39. C	Phonics	0 1
40. D	Phonics	0 1
Grammar		
41. B	Simple Past	0 1
42. A	Simple Past	0 1
43. B	Active and Passive Voice	0 1
44. A	Subject/Verb Agreement	0 1
45. B	Adverb Clauses of Time	0 1
46. A	Relative Clauses	0 1
47. A	Infinitives	0 1
48. B	Conjunctions	0 1
49. C	Comparison Structures	0 1
50. B	Quoted Speech	0 1
Writing		(Score with rubric.)
51–60.	Letter Writing	_____
	Writing a Description	
	Use Descriptive Words	
	Sentence Structure	
	Punctuation and	
	Capitalization	
Oral Reading Fluency		(Circle one.)
61–70.	Speed	0 1 2
	Accuracy	0 1 2
	Expression	0 1 2
	Intonation	0 1 2
	Self-correction	0 1 2

_____ ÷ **70** x **100** = _____
(Student's Total Score)   (Total Possible Points)   (Student's Percent Score)

Midterm Test Answer Key and Tested Skills Chart

Answer	Tested Skill	Score
Listening and Reading Comprehension		(Circle one.)
1. C	Listening/Answering Questions	0 1
2. B	Listening/Identify Cause and Effect	0 1
3. C	Listening/Answer Questions/Character Motivation	0 1
4. A	Listening/Character	0 1
5. B	Listening/Comprehension	0 1
6. C	Listening/Answer Questions	0 1
7. B	Listening/Theme	0 1
8. D	Listening/Draw Conclusions	0 1
9. B	Comprehension	0 1
10. B	Identify Cause and Effect	0 1
11. C	Character	0 1
12. D	Plot/Character	0 1
13. C	Comprehension	0 1
14. B	Comprehension	0 1
15. D	Compare	0 1
16. B	Reading Charts	0 1
Vocabulary		
17. B	Literary Words	0 1
18. D	Literary Words	0 1
19. C	Literary Words	0 1
20. A	Literary Words	0 1
21. C	Literary Words	0 1
22. A	Literary Words	0 1
23. A	Literary Words	0 1
24. A	Key Words	0 1
25. D	Key Words	0 1
26. B	Key Words	0 1
27. D	Key Words	0 1
28. C	Key Words	0 1
29. B	Key Words	0 1
30. C	Academic Words	0 1
31. B	Academic Words	0 1
32. A	Academic Words	0 1
33. B	Academic Words	0 1

Answer	Tested Skill	Score
Word Study		(Circle one.)
34. A	Word Origins	0 1
35. A	Simple Past	0 1
36. C	Homophones	0 1
37. D	Prefixes	0 1
38. D	Spelling	0 1
39. B	Prefixes	0 1
40. A	Prefixes	0 1
Grammar		
41. C	Word Order	0 1
42. A	Gerunds	0 1
43. C	Infinitives	0 1
44. C	Comparison Structures	0 1
45. D	Subject/Verb Agreement	0 1
46. B	Active and Passive Voice	0 1
47. D	Independent and Dependent Clauses	0 1
48. A	Nouns	0 1
49. A	Simple Past	0 1
50. C	Gerunds	0 1
Writing		(Score with rubric.)
51-60.	Select a Focus	_____
	Write a Brief Description	
	Create a Composition	
	Answer Questions	
	Sentence Structure	
	Punctuation and Capitalization	
Oral Reading Fluency		(Circle one.)
61-70.	Speed	0 1 2
	Accuracy	0 1 2
	Expression	0 1 2
	Intonation	0 1 2
	Self-correction	0 1 2

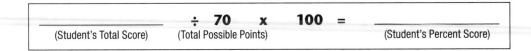

_____	÷ **70**	x **100**	=	_____
(Student's Total Score)	(Total Possible Points)			(Student's Percent Score)

Posttest Answer Key and Tested Skills Chart

Answer	Tested Skill	Score
Listening and Reading Comprehension		(Circle one.)
1. D	Listening/Answer Questions	0 1
2. B	Listening/Answer Questions	0 1
3. A	Listening/Character Motivation	0 1
4. C	Listening/Character Motivation/Identify Cause and Effect	0 1
5. D	Listening/Comprehension	0 1
6. C	Listening/Answer Questions	0 1
7. D	Listening/Comprehension	0 1
8. B	Listening/Comprehension	0 1
9. D	Make Inferences	0 1
10. A	Make Inferences/Answer Questions	0 1
11. C	Make Inferences/Answer Questions	0 1
12. B	Make Inferences/Answer Questions	0 1
13. B	Comprehension	0 1
14. C	Answer Questions	0 1
15. C	Comprehension	0 1
16. A	Make Inferences/Paraphrase	0 1
Vocabulary		
17. D	Literary Words	0 1
18. B	Literary Words	0 1
19. D	Literary Words	0 1
20. B	Literary Words	0 1
21. A	Literary Words	0 1
22. C	Literary Words	0 1
23. C	Literary Words	0 1
24. B	Key Words	0 1
25. A	Key Words	0 1
26. C	Key Words	0 1
27. A	Key Words	0 1
28. D	Key Words	0 1
29. B	Key Words	0 1
30. C	Academic Words	0 1
31. D	Academic Words	0 1
32. C	Academic Words	0 1
33. A	Academic Words	0 1

Answer	Tested Skill	Score
Word Study		(Circle one.)
34. C	Plurals	0 1
35. A	Simple Past	0 1
36. A	Prefixes	0 1
37. D	Compound Nouns	0 1
38. B	Suffixes	0 1
39. C	Phonics	0 1
40. D	Phonics	0 1
Grammar		
41. D	Simple Past	0 1
42. B	Simple Past	0 1
43. C	Active and Passive Voice	0 1
44. A	Subject/Verb Agreement	0 1
45. B	Adverb Clauses of Time	0 1
46. B	Relative Clauses	0 1
47. D	Infinitives	0 1
48. A	Conjunctions	0 1
49. B	Comparison Structures	0 1
50. B	Quoted Speech	0 1
Writing		(Score with rubric.)
51-60.	Write a Persuasive Letter Consistent Focus Order and Structure Sentence Structure Punctuation and Capitalization	_____
Oral Reading Fluency		(Circle one.)
61-70.	Speed	0 1 2
	Accuracy	0 1 2
	Expression	0 1 2
	Intonation	0 1 2
	Self-correction	0 1 2

_____ ÷ **70** x **100** = _____
(Student's Total Score) (Total Possible Points)   (Student's Percent Score)

Unit 1 Reading 1 Test Answer Key and Tested Skills Chart

Answer	Tested Skill	Score
Literary Words		(Circle one.)
1. C	Literary Words	0 1
2. B	Literary Words	0 1
3. D	Literary Words	0 1
4. B	Literary Words	0 1
5. D	Literary Words	0 1
6. A	Literary Words	0 1
Academic Words		
7. D	Academic Words	0 1
8. D	Academic Words	0 1
9. B	Academic Words	0 1
10. B	Academic Words	0 1
Word Study		
11. A	Word Analysis	0 1
12. C	Word Analysis	0 1
13. D	Word Analysis	0 1
14. B	Word Analysis	0 1
15. A	Word Analysis	0 1
16. C	Word Analysis	0 1

Answer	Tested Skill	Score
Reading		(Circle one.)
17. A	Comprehension	0 1
18. B	Comprehension	0 1
19. B	Recognize Sequence	0 1
20. D	Identify Cause and Effect	0 1
21. C	Make Inferences	0 1
22. D	Identify Author's Purpose	0 1
23. B	Identify Details	0 1
Grammar		
24. C	Order of Adjectives	0 1
25. A	Order of Adjectives	0 1
26. B	Order of Adjectives	0 1
27. D	Order of Adjectives	0 1
28. A	Order of Adjectives	0 1
29. C	Order of Adjectives	0 1
30. D	Order of Adjectives	0 1

_____ ÷ 30 × 100 = _____
(Student's Total Score) (Total Possible Points) (Student's Percent Score)

Answer	Tested Skill	Score (Circle one.)
Key Words		
1. D	Key Words	0 1
2. D	Key Words	0 1
3. A	Key Words	0 1
4. C	Key Words	0 1
5. C	Key Words	0 1
6. A	Key Words	0 1
Academic Words		
7. C	Academic Words	0 1
8. D	Academic Words	0 1
9. A	Academic Words	0 1
10. C	Academic Words	0 1
11. B	Academic Words	0 1
Word Study		
12. B	Word Analysis	0 1
13. D	Word Analysis	0 1
14. B	Word Analysis	0 1
15. D	Word Analysis	0 1
16. A	Word Analysis	0 1
17. A	Word Analysis	0 1

Answer	Tested Skill	Score (Circle one.)
Reading		
18. B	Identify Details	0 1
19. D	Identify Details	0 1
20. D	Identify Details	0 1
21. A	Identify Main Idea	0 1
22. D	Identify Main Idea	0 1
23. B	Identify Details	0 1
24. A	Identify Details	0 1
Grammar		
25. D	Comparison Structures	0 1
26. B	Comparison Structures	0 1
27. C	Comparison Structures	0 1
28. B	Comparison Structures	0 1
29. A	Comparison Structures	0 1
30. B	Comparison Structures	0 1

_____ ÷ **30** x **100** = _____
(Student's Total Score) (Total Possible Points) (Student's Percent Score)

Unit 1 Reading 3 Test Answer Key and Tested Skills Chart

Answer	Tested Skill	Score
Literary Words		(Circle one.)
1. B	Literary Words	0 1
2. C	Literary Words	0 1
3. B	Literary Words	0 1
4. C	Literary Words	0 1
5. D	Literary Words	0 1
Academic Words		
6. B	Academic Words	0 1
7. D	Academic Words	0 1
8. C	Academic Words	0 1
9. B	Academic Words	0 1
10. A	Academic Words	0 1
Word Study		
11. C	Word Analysis	0 1
12. D	Word Analysis	0 1
13. B	Word Analysis	0 1
14. A	Word Analysis	0 1
15. C	Word Analysis	0 1
16. A	Word Analysis	0 1

Answer	Tested Skill	Score
Reading		(Circle one.)
17. D	Comprehension	0 1
18. C	Comprehension	0 1
19. A	Identify Details	0 1
20. C	Make Inferences	0 1
21. B	Identify Details	0 1
22. D	Identify Main Idea	0 1
23. D	Genre	0 1
Grammar		
24. B	Simple and Compound Sentences	0 1
25. C	Simple and Compound Sentences	0 1
26. A	Simple and Compound Sentences	0 1
27. D	Simple and Compound Sentences	0 1
28. B	Simple and Compound Sentences	0 1
29. D	Simple and Compound Sentences	0 1
30. B	Simple and Compound Sentences	0 1

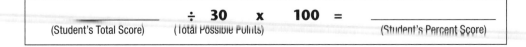

_____ ÷ **30** x **100** = _____
(Student's Total Score) (Total Possible Points) (Student's Percent Score)

Unit 1 Reading 4 Test Answer Key and Tested Skills Chart

Answer	Tested Skill	Score
Key Words		(Circle one.)
1. C	Key Words	0 1
2. D	Key Words	0 1
3. C	Key Words	0 1
4. A	Key Words	0 1
5. D	Key Words	0 1
6. B	Key Words	0 1
Academic Words		
7. D	Academic Words	0 1
8. B	Academic Words	0 1
9. B	Academic Words	0 1
10. C	Academic Words	0 1
11. A	Academic Words	0 1
12. D	Academic Words	0 1
Word Study		
13. B	Word Analysis	0 1
14. D	Word Analysis	0 1
15. B	Word Analysis	0 1
16. C	Word Analysis	0 1
17. C	Word Analysis	0 1
18. D	Word Analysis	0 1

Answer	Tested Skill	Score
Reading		(Circle one.)
19. D	Compare and Contrast	0 1
20. A	Identify Details	0 1
21. D	Identify Details	0 1
22. A	Identify Cause and Effect	0 1
23. C	Identify Cause and Effect	0 1
24. A	Identify Cause and Effect	0 1
25. A	Identify Details	0 1
Grammar		
26. D	Subject/Verb Agreement	0 1
27. A	Subject/Verb Agreement	0 1
28. B	Subject/Verb Agreement	0 1
29. C	Subject/Verb Agreement	0 1
30. B	Subject/Verb Agreement	0 1

_____ ÷ **30** x **100** = _____
(Student's Total Score) (Total Possible Points) (Student's Percent Score)

Unit 2 Reading 1 Test Answer Key and Tested Skills Chart

Answer	Tested Skill	Score
Literary Words		(Circle one.)
1. A	Literary Words	0 1
2. D	Literary Words	0 1
3. D	Literary Words	0 1
4. A	Literary Words	0 1
5. D	Literary Words	0 1
6. C	Literary Words	0 1
Academic Words		
7. A	Academic Words	0 1
8. A	Academic Words	0 1
9. B	Academic Words	0 1
10. D	Academic Words	0 1
11. D	Academic Words	0 1
12. D	Academic Words	0 1
13. A	Word Analysis	0 1
14. D	Word Analysis	0 1
15. C	Word Analysis	0 1
16. B	Word Analysis	0 1

Answer	Tested Skill	Score
Reading		(Circle one.)
17. D	Comprehension	0 1
18. C	Comprehension	0 1
19. A	Plot	0 1
20. A	Identify Cause and Effect	0 1
21. B	Make Inferences	0 1
22. D	Identify Author's Purpose	0 1
23. B	Identify Details	0 1
Grammar		
24. B	Simple Past	0 1
25. C	Simple Past	0 1
26. B	Simple Past	0 1
27. C	Simple Past	0 1
28. A	Simple Past	0 1
29. D	Simple Past	0 1
30. B	Simple Past	0 1

_____ ÷ **30** x **100** = _____
(Student's Total Score) (Total Possible Points) (Student's Percent Score)

Answer	Tested Skill	Score
Key Words		(Circle one.)
1. D	Key Words	0 1
2. C	Key Words	0 1
3. D	Key Words	0 1
4. B	Key Words	0 1
5. A	Key Words	0 1
6. C	Key Words	0 1
Academic Words		
7. C	Academic Words	0 1
8. B	Academic Words	0 1
9. D	Academic Words	0 1
10. C	Academic Words	0 1
11. D	Academic Words	0 1
Word Study		
12. A	Word Analysis	0 1
13. B	Word Analysis	0 1
14. C	Word Analysis	0 1
15. D	Word Analysis	0 1
16. B	Word Analysis	0 1

Answer	Tested Skill	Score
Reading		(Circle one.)
17. D	Identify Main Idea	0 1
18. C	Identify Main Idea	0 1
19. B	Identify Details	0 1
20. B	Identify Main Idea	0 1
21. A	Identify Details	0 1
22. B	Identify Main Idea	0 1
23. D	Identify Details	0 1
Grammar		
24. C	Active and Passive Voice	0 1
25. C	Active and Passive Voice	0 1
26. D	Active and Passive Voice	0 1
27. B	Active and Passive Voice	0 1
28. A	Active and Passive Voice	0 1
29. C	Active and Passive Voice	0 1
30. D	Active and Passive Voice	0 1

_____ ÷ **30** x **100** = _____
(Student's Total Score) (Total Possible Points) (Student's Percent Score)

Unit 2 Reading 3 Test Answer Key and Tested Skills Chart

Answer	Tested Skill	Score
Key Words		(Circle one.)
1. C	Key Words	0 1
2. A	Key Words	0 1
3. B	Key Words	0 1
4. B	Key Words	0 1
5. D	Key Words	0 1
6. B	Key Words	0 1
Academic Words		
7. C	Academic Words	0 1
8. D	Academic Words	0 1
9. A	Academic Words	0 1
10. D	Academic Words	0 1
Word Study		
11. B	Word Analysis	0 1
12. A	Word Analysis	0 1
13. B	Word Analysis	0 1
14. D	Word Analysis	0 1
15. C	Word Analysis	0 1
16. A	Word Analysis	0 1

Answer	Tested Skill	Score
Reading		(Circle one.)
17. C	Identify Details	0 1
18. C	Identify Main Idea	0 1
19. A	Identify Details	0 1
20. A	Identify Main Idea	0 1
21. C	Identify Main Idea	0 1
22. A	Identify Main Idea	0 1
23. A	Comprehension	0 1
Grammar		
24. B	Prenominal and Postnominal Adjectives	0 1
25. A	Prenominal and Postnominal Adjectives	0 1
26. D	Prenominal and Postnominal Adjectives	0 1
27. C	Prenominal and Postnominal Adjectives	0 1
28. B	Prenominal and Postnominal Adjectives	0 1
29. A	Prenominal and Postnominal Adjectives	0 1
30. D	Prenominal and Postnominal Adjectives	0 1

_____ ÷ **30** x **100** = _____
(Student's Total Score)   (Total Possible Points)   (Student's Percent Score)

LEVEL B

Unit 2 Reading 4 Test Answer Key and Tested Skills Chart

Answer	Tested Skill	Score
Literary Words		(Circle one.)
1. B	Literary Words	0 1
2. D	Literary Words	0 1
3. B	Literary Words	0 1
4. C	Literary Words	0 1
5. C	Literary Words	0 1
6. B	Literary Words	0 1
Academic Words		
7. D	Academic Words	0 1
8. D	Academic Words	0 1
9. A	Academic Words	0 1
10. D	Academic Words	0 1
11. D	Academic Words	0 1
Word Study		
12. B	Word Analysis	0 1
13. A	Word Analysis	0 1
14. D	Word Analysis	0 1
15. C	Word Analysis	0 1
16. C	Word Analysis	0 1

Answer	Tested Skill	Score
Reading		(Circle one.)
17. C	Identify Details	0 1
18. D	Comprehension	0 1
19. A	Point of View	0 1
20. B	Identify Details	0 1
21. A	Identify Details	0 1
22. B	Comprehension	0 1
23. D	Identify Details	0 1
Grammar		
24. C	Adverb Clauses of Time	0 1
25. B	Adverb Clauses of Time	0 1
26. B	Adverb Clauses of Time	0 1
27. B	Adverb Clauses of Time	0 1
28. D	Adverb Clauses of Time	0 1
29. B	Adverb Clauses of Time	0 1
30. C	Adverb Clauses of Time	0 1

_____ ÷ **30** x **100** = _____
(Student's Total Score) (Total Possible Points) (Student's Percent Score)

Copyright © by Pearson Education, Inc.

Answer	Tested Skill	Score
Key Words		(Circle one.)
1. D	Key Words	0 1
2. B	Key Words	0 1
3. C	Key Words	0 1
4. C	Key Words	0 1
5. C	Key Words	0 1
6. B	Key Words	0 1
Academic Words		
7. B	Academic Words	0 1
8. C	Academic Words	0 1
9. A	Academic Words	0 1
10. C	Academic Words	0 1
11. C	Academic Words	0 1
Word Study		
12. A	Word Analysis	0 1
13. B	Word Analysis	0 1
14. D	Word Analysis	0 1
15. D	Word Analysis	0 1
16. B	Word Analysis	0 1
17. C	Word Analysis	0 1

Answer	Tested Skill	Score
Reading		(Circle one.)
18. D	Comprehension	0 1
19. A	Identify Main Idea	0 1
20. B	Identify Details	0 1
21. D	Comprehension	0 1
22. A	Making Inferences	0 1
23. D	Identify Details	0 1
Grammar		
24. D	Independent and Dependent Clauses	0 1
25. C	Independent and Dependent Clauses	0 1
26. B	Independent and Dependent Clauses	0 1
27. A	Independent and Dependent Clauses	0 1
28. C	Independent and Dependent Clauses	0 1
29. D	Independent and Dependent Clauses	0 1
30. B	Independent and Dependent Clauses	0 1

_____ ÷ **30** x **100** = _____
(Student's Total Score) (Total Possible Points) (Student's Percent Score)

Answer	Tested Skill	Score
Literary Words		(Circle one.)
1. B	Literary Words	0 1
2. D	Literary Words	0 1
3. B	Literary Words	0 1
4. B	Literary Words	0 1
5. A	Literary Words	0 1
6. D	Literary Words	0 1
Academic Words		
7. D	Academic Words	0 1
8. B	Academic Words	0 1
9. C	Academic Words	0 1
10. A	Academic Words	0 1
11. C	Academic Words	0 1
Word Study		
12. C	Word Analysis	0 1
13. D	Word Analysis	0 1
14. B	Word Analysis	0 1
15. A	Word Analysis	0 1
16. D	Word Analysis	0 1
17. B	Word Analysis	0 1

Answer	Tested Skill	Score
Reading		(Circle one.)
18. D	Identify Details	0 1
19. C	Identify Details	0 1
20. B	Identify Details	0 1
21. B	Genre	0 1
22. D	Genre	0 1
23. C	Make Inferences	0 1
Grammar		
24. B	Gerunds	0 1
25. C	Gerunds	0 1
26. D	Gerunds	0 1
27. A	Gerunds	0 1
28. C	Gerunds	0 1
29. D	Gerunds	0 1
30. A	Gerunds	0 1

_____ ÷ **30** x **100** = _____
(Student's Total Score) (Total Possible Points) (Student's Percent Score)

Answer	Tested Skill	Score (Circle one.)
Literary Words		
1. B	Literary Words	0 1
2. C	Literary Words	0 1
3. A	Literary Words	0 1
4. B	Literary Words	0 1
5. A	Literary Words	0 1
6. C	Literary Words	0 1
Academic Words		
7. C	Academic Words	0 1
8. A	Academic Words	0 1
9. C	Academic Words	0 1
10. B	Academic Words	0 1
11. D	Academic Words	0 1
Word Study		
12. B	Word Analysis	0 1
13. A	Word Analysis	0 1
14. D	Word Analysis	0 1
15. C	Word Analysis	0 1
16. C	Word Analysis	0 1
17. C	Word Analysis	0 1

Answer	Tested Skill	Score (Circle one.)
Reading		
18. A	Identify Details	0 1
19. C	Identify Main Idea	0 1
20. D	Comprehension	0 1
21. C	Comprehension	0 1
22. C	Identify Details	0 1
23. D	Comprehension	0 1
Grammar		
24. C	Infinitives	0 1
25. B	Infinitives	0 1
26. A	Infinitives	0 1
27. D	Infinitives	0 1
28. B	Infinitives	0 1
29. B	Infinitives	0 1
30. C	Infinitives	0 1

_____ ÷ **30** x **100** = _____
(Student's Total Score)   (Total Possible Points)   (Student's Percent Score)

Answer	Tested Skill	Score
Key Words		(Circle one.)
1. B	Key Words	0 1
2. A	Key Words	0 1
3. C	Key Words	0 1
4. B	Key Words	0 1
5. C	Key Words	0 1
6. A	Key Words	0 1
Academic Words		
7. C	Academic Words	0 1
8. D	Academic Words	0 1
9. A	Academic Words	0 1
10. A	Academic Words	0 1
11. C	Academic Words	0 1
Word Study		
12. A	Word Analysis	0 1
13. C	Word Analysis	0 1
14. D	Word Analysis	0 1
15. B	Word Analysis	0 1
16. C	Word Analysis	0 1
17. B	Word Analysis	0 1

Answer	Tested Skill	Score
Reading		(Circle one.)
18. D	Comprehension	0 1
19. D	Comprehension	0 1
20. A	Identify Details	0 1
21. B	Identify Details	0 1
22. C	Comprehension	0 1
23. A	Make Inferences	0 1
Grammar		
24. B	Expressions of Quantity	0 1
25. D	Expressions of Quantity	0 1
26. B	Expressions of Quantity	0 1
27. A	Expressions of Quantity	0 1
28. D	Expressions of Quantity	0 1
29. C	Expressions of Quantity	0 1
30. B	Expressions of Quantity	0 1

$$\underline{\hspace{3cm}} \div \; \mathbf{30} \quad \mathbf{x} \quad \mathbf{100} \; = \; \underline{\hspace{3cm}}$$

(Student's Total Score)   (Total Possible Points)   (Student's Percent Score)

LEVEL B

Unit 4 Reading 1 Test Answer Key and Tested Skills Chart

Answer	Tested Skill	Score (Circle one.)
Key Words		
1. C	Key Words	0 1
2. B	Key Words	0 1
3. C	Key Words	0 1
4. A	Key Words	0 1
5. C	Key Words	0 1
6. D	Key Words	0 1
Academic Words		
7. A	Academic Words	0 1
8. D	Academic Words	0 1
9. D	Academic Words	0 1
10. A	Academic Words	0 1
11. B	Academic Words	0 1
Word Study		
12. C	Word Analysis	0 1
13. D	Word Analysis	0 1
14. B	Word Analysis	0 1
15. A	Word Analysis	0 1
16. B	Word Analysis	0 1

Answer	Tested Skill	Score (Circle one.)
Reading		
17. D	Comprehension	0 1
18. B	Identify Main Idea	0 1
19. C	Comprehension	0 1
20. C	Make Inferences	0 1
21. B	Preview and Predict	0 1
22. A	Identify Details	0 1
23. A	Make Inferences	0 1
Grammar		
24. D	Present Perfect	0 1
25. C	Present Perfect	0 1
26. B	Present Perfect	0 1
27. A	Present Perfect	0 1
28. C	Present Perfect	0 1
29. D	Present Perfect	0 1
30. C	Present Perfect	0 1

_____ ÷ **30** x **100** = _____
(Student's Total Score) (Total Possible Points)   (Student's Percent Score)

Unit 4 Reading 2 Test Answer Key and Tested Skills Chart

Answer	Tested Skill	Score
Literary Words		(Circle one.)
1. C	Literary Words	0 1
2. D	Literary Words	0 1
3. A	Literary Words	0 1
4. D	Literary Words	0 1
5. C	Literary Words	0 1
6. A	Literary Words	0 1
Academic Words		
7. A	Academic Words	0 1
8. B	Academic Words	0 1
9. D	Academic Words	0 1
10. C	Academic Words	0 1
11. A	Academic Words	0 1
12. B	Academic Words	0 1
Word Study		
13. A	Word Analysis	0 1
14. B	Word Analysis	0 1
15. D	Word Analysis	0 1
16. C	Word Analysis	0 1

Answer	Tested Skill	Score
Reading		(Circle one.)
17. B	Comprehension	0 1
18. B	Identify Details	0 1
19. D	Identify Cause and Effect	0 1
20. D	Comprehension	0 1
21. C	Comprehension	0 1
22. D	Preview and Predict	0 1
23. B	Identify Main Idea	0 1
Grammar		
24. A	Future (with *will*)	0 1
25. C	Future (with *will*)	0 1
26. B	Future (with *will*)	0 1
27. C	Future (with *will*)	0 1
28. B	Future (with *will*)	0 1
29. D	Future (with *will*)	0 1
30. A	Future (with *will*)	0 1

_____ ÷ **30** x **100** = _____
(Student's Total Score)   (Total Possible Points)   (Student's Percent Score)

Answer	Tested Skill	Score
Key Words		(Circle one.)
1. C	Key Words	0 1
2. B	Key Words	0 1
3. A	Key Words	0 1
4. D	Key Words	0 1
5. A	Key Words	0 1
6. C	Key Words	0 1
Academic Words		
7. A	Academic Words	0 1
8. C	Academic Words	0 1
9. B	Academic Words	0 1
10. D	Academic Words	0 1
11. D	Academic Words	0 1
12. A	Academic Words	0 1
Word Study		
13. B	Word Analysis	0 1
14. D	Word Analysis	0 1
15. D	Word Analysis	0 1
16. C	Word Analysis	0 1

Answer	Tested Skill	Score
Reading		(Circle one.)
17. B	Identify Main Idea	0 1
18. C	Identify Details	0 1
19. A	Comprehension	0 1
20. D	Identify Details	0 1
21. B	Comprehension	0 1
22. D	Recognize Sequence	0 1
23. C	Comprehension	0 1
Grammar		
24. B	Conjunctions (*and, but, or*)	0 1
25. C	Conjunctions (*and, but, or*)	0 1
26. D	Conjunctions (*and, but, or*)	0 1
27. A	Conjunctions (*and, but, or*)	0 1
28. C	Conjunctions (*and, but, or*)	0 1
29. A	Conjunctions (*and, but, or*)	0 1
30. D	Conjunctions (*and, but, or*)	0 1

_____ ÷ **30** x **100** = _____
(Student's Total Score) (Total Possible Points) (Student's Percent Score)

Answer	Tested Skill	Score
Literary Words		(Circle one.)
1. D	Literary Words	0 1
2. B	Literary Words	0 1
3. C	Literary Words	0 1
4. D	Literary Words	0 1
5. B	Literary Words	0 1
6. B	Literary Words	0 1
Academic Words		
7. C	Academic Words	0 1
8. A	Academic Words	0 1
9. B	Academic Words	0 1
10. B	Academic Words	0 1
11. D	Academic Words	0 1
Word Study		
12. B	Word Analysis	0 1
13. A	Word Analysis	0 1
14. A	Word Analysis	0 1
15. C	Word Analysis	0 1
16. D	Word Analysis	0 1

Answer	Tested Skill	Score
Reading		(Circle one.)
17. A	Identify Details	0 1
18. B	Summarize	0 1
19. D	Recognize Sequence	0 1
20. B	Make Inferences	0 1
21. C	Genre	0 1
22. D	Make Inferences	0 1
23. A	Compare and Contrast	0 1
Grammar		
24. C	Possessive Adjective	0 1
25. A	Possessive Adjective	0 1
26. D	Possessive Adjective	0 1
27. B	Possessive Adjective	0 1
28. C	Possessive Adjective	0 1
29. A	Possessive Adjective	0 1
30. B	Possessive Adjective	0 1

_____ ÷ **30** x **100** = _____
(Student's Total Score)   (Total Possible Points)   (Student's Percent Score)

Unit 5 Reading 1 Test Answer Key and Tested Skills Chart

Answer	Tested Skill	Score
Literary Words		(Circle one.)
1. D	Literary Words	0 1
2. B	Literary Words	0 1
3. C	Literary Words	0 1
4. A	Literary Words	0 1
5. B	Literary Words	0 1
6. C	Literary Words	0 1
Academic Words		
7. C	Academic Words	0 1
8. A	Academic Words	0 1
9. A	Academic Words	0 1
10. C	Academic Words	0 1
11. B	Academic Words	0 1
Word Study		
12. A	Word Analysis	0 1
13. B	Word Analysis	0 1
14. D	Word Analysis	0 1
15. A	Word Analysis	0 1
16. A	Word Analysis	0 1

Answer	Tested Skill	Score
Reading		(Circle one.)
17. B	Recognize Sequence	0 1
18. D	Summarize	0 1
19. D	Identify Details	0 1
20. B	Comprehension	0 1
21. D	Identify Details	0 1
22. C	Simile	0 1
23. A	Comprehension	0 1
Grammar		
24. B	Past Perfect	0 1
25. B	Past Perfect	0 1
26. D	Past Perfect	0 1
27. B	Past Perfect	0 1
28. C	Past Perfect	0 1
29. C	Past Perfect	0 1
30. C	Past Perfect	0 1

_____ ÷ **30** x **100** = _____
(Student's Total Score)   (Total Possible Points)   (Student's Percent Score)

Answer	Tested Skill	Score
Key Words		(Circle one.)
1. D	Key Words	0 1
2. C	Key Words	0 1
3. A	Key Words	0 1
4. D	Key Words	0 1
5. C	Key Words	0 1
6. C	Key Words	0 1
Academic Words		
7. C	Academic Words	0 1
8. B	Academic Words	0 1
9. D	Academic Words	0 1
10. D	Academic Words	0 1
11. A	Academic Words	0 1
12. B	Academic Words	0 1
Word Study		
13. D	Word Analysis	0 1
14. A	Word Analysis	0 1
15. C	Word Analysis	0 1
16. D	Word Analysis	0 1

Answer	Tested Skill	Score
Reading		(Circle one.)
17. B	Use Visuals	0 1
18. A	Use Visuals	0 1
19. D	Comprehension	0 1
20. C	Supporting Details	0 1
21. D	Comprehension	0 1
22. C	Comprehension	0 1
23. A	Comprehension	0 1
Grammar		
24. A	Imperatives	0 1
25. C	Imperatives	0 1
26. B	Imperatives	0 1
27. D	Imperatives	0 1
28. A	Imperatives	0 1
29. C	Imperatives	0 1
30. B	Imperatives	0 1

_____ ÷ **30** x **100** = _____
(Student's Total Score)   (Total Possible Points)   (Student's Percent Score)

Answer	Tested Skill	Score
Key Words		(Circle one.)
1. A	Key Words	0 1
2. A	Key Words	0 1
3. D	Key Words	0 1
4. B	Key Words	0 1
5. C	Key Words	0 1
6. C	Key Words	0 1
Academic Words		
7. B	Academic Words	0 1
8. D	Academic Words	0 1
9. A	Academic Words	0 1
10. B	Academic Words	0 1
11. C	Academic Words	0 1
Word Study		
12. C	Word Analysis	0 1
13. A	Word Analysis	0 1
14. B	Word Analysis	0 1
15. C	Word Analysis	0 1
16. D	Word Analysis	0 1

Answer	Tested Skill	Score
Reading		(Circle one.)
17. C	Comprehension	0 1
18. B	Identify Details	0 1
19. B	Identify Main Idea	0 1
20. C	Identify Details	0 1
21. A	Compare and Contrast	0 1
22. B	Recognize Sequence	0 1
23. B	Identify Cause and Effect	0 1
Grammar		
24. C	Modals (*could, might*)	0 1
25. B	Modals (*could, might*)	0 1
26. D	Modals (*could, might*)	0 1
27. C	Modals (*could, might*)	0 1
28. A	Modals (*could, might*)	0 1
29. A	Modals (*could, might*)	0 1
30. B	Modals (*could, might*)	0 1

_____ ÷ **30** x **100** = _____
(Student's Total Score) (Total Possible Points) (Student's Percent Score)

Answer	Tested Skill	Score
Literary Words		(Circle one.)
1. B	Literary Words	0 1
2. D	Literary Words	0 1
3. D	Literary Words	0 1
4. C	Literary Words	0 1
5. C	Literary Words	0 1
6. A	Literary Words	0 1
Academic Words		
7. D	Academic Words	0 1
8. B	Academic Words	0 1
9. A	Academic Words	0 1
10. C	Academic Words	0 1
11. A	Academic Words	0 1
12. B	Academic Words	0 1
Word Study		
13. B	Word Analysis	0 1
14. A	Word Analysis	0 1
15. C	Word Analysis	0 1
16. C	Word Analysis	0 1
17. B	Word Analysis	0 1

Answer	Tested Skill	Score
Reading		(Circle one.)
18. C	Recognize Sequence	0 1
19. C	Identify Details	0 1
20. D	Comprehension	0 1
21. A	Identify Details	0 1
22. B	Character	0 1
23. D	Make Inferences	0 1
Grammar		
24. D	Comparison Structures	0 1
25. D	Comparison Structures	0 1
26. B	Comparison Structures	0 1
27. D	Comparison Structures	0 1
28. B	Comparison Structures	0 1
29. B	Comparison Structures	0 1
30. C	Comparison Structures	0 1

_____ ÷ **30** x **100** = _____
(Student's Total Score) (Total Possible Points) (Student's Percent Score)

LEVEL B
Unit 6 Reading 1 Test Answer Key and Tested Skills Chart

Answer	Tested Skill	Score
Literary Words		(Circle one.)
1. A	Literary Words	0 1
2. D	Literary Words	0 1
3. C	Literary Words	0 1
4. A	Literary Words	0 1
5. C	Literary Words	0 1
6. B	Literary Words	0 1
Academic Words		
7. A	Academic Words	0 1
8. B	Academic Words	0 1
9. D	Academic Words	0 1
10. D	Academic Words	0 1
11. A	Academic Words	0 1
12. B	Academic Words	0 1
Word Study		
13. B	Word Analysis	0 1
14. A	Word Analysis	0 1
15. B	Word Analysis	0 1
16. C	Word Analysis	0 1
17. D	Word Analysis	0 1

Answer	Tested Skill	Score
Reading		(Circle one.)
18. B	Comprehension	0 1
19. A	Summarize	0 1
20. A	Identify Details	0 1
21. C	Identify Details	0 1
22. A	Comprehension	0 1
23. D	Compare and Contrast	0 1
Grammar		
24. C	Modals (ability, necessity, permission)	0 1
25. A	Modals (ability, necessity, permission)	0 1
26. B	Modals (ability, necessity, permission)	0 1
27. D	Modals (ability, necessity, permission)	0 1
28. D	Modals (ability, necessity, permission)	0 1
29. D	Modals (ability, necessity, permission)	0 1
30. C	Modals (ability, necessity, permission)	0 1

_____ ÷ **30** x **100** = _____
(Student's Total Score) (Total Possible Points) (Student's Percent Score)

Unit 6 Reading 2 Test Answer Key and Tested Skills Chart

Answer	Tested Skill	Score
Key Words		(Circle one.)
1. D	Key Words	0 1
2. C	Key Words	0 1
3. C	Key Words	0 1
4. C	Key Words	0 1
5. D	Key Words	0 1
6. B	Key Words	0 1
Academic Words		
7. B	Academic Words	0 1
8. A	Academic Words	0 1
9. D	Academic Words	0 1
10. B	Academic Words	0 1
11. C	Academic Words	0 1
Word Study		
12. C	Word Analysis	0 1
13. B	Word Analysis	0 1
14. A	Word Analysis	0 1
15. C	Word Analysis	0 1
16. D	Word Analysis	0 1
17. B	Word Analysis	0 1

Answer	Tested Skill	Score
Reading		(Circle one.)
18. B	Comprehension	0 1
19. B	Comprehension	0 1
20. D	Identify Details	0 1
21. D	Identify Details	0 1
22. D	Identify Details	0 1
23. B	Identify Details	0 1
Grammar		
24. A	Adjectives ending in *-ing* and *-ed*	0 1
25. C	Adjectives ending in *-ing* and *-ed*	0 1
26. B	Adjectives ending in *-ing* and *-ed*	0 1
27. C	Adjectives ending in *-ing* and *-ed*	0 1
28. B	Adjectives ending in *-ing* and *-ed*	0 1
29. A	Adjectives ending in *-ing* and *-ed*	0 1
30. D	Adjectives ending in *-ing* and *-ed*	0 1

_____ ÷ **30** x **100** = _____
(Student's Total Score)   (Total Possible Points)   (Student's Percent Score)

Answer	Tested Skill	Score
Literary Words		(Circle one.)
1. A	Literary Words	0 1
2. C	Literary Words	0 1
3. B	Literary Words	0 1
4. C	Literary Words	0 1
5. D	Literary Words	0 1
6. C	Literary Words	0 1
Academic Words		
7. A	Academic Words	0 1
8. D	Academic Words	0 1
9. C	Academic Words	0 1
10. A	Academic Words	0 1
11. B	Academic Words	0 1
Word Study		
12. D	Word Analysis	0 1
13. B	Word Analysis	0 1
14. C	Word Analysis	0 1
15. D	Word Analysis	0 1
16. A	Word Analysis	0 1
17. B	Word Analysis	0 1

Answer	Tested Skill	Score
Reading		(Circle one.)
18. C	Plot	0 1
19. D	Identify Details	0 1
20. A	Simile	0 1
21. B	Identify Details	0 1
22. D	Plot	0 1
23. B	Identify Cause and Effect	0 1
Grammar		
24. B	Quoted Speech	0 1
25. D	Quoted Speech	0 1
26. C	Quoted Speech	0 1
27. C	Quoted Speech	0 1
28. D	Quoted Speech	0 1
29. A	Quoted Speech	0 1
30. B	Quoted Speech	0 1

_____	÷ **30**	x **100**	=	_____
(Student's Total Score)	(Total Possible Points)			(Student's Percent Score)

Answer	Tested Skill	Score
Key Words		(Circle one.)
1. B	Key Words	0 1
2. B	Key Words	0 1
3. A	Key Words	0 1
4. D	Key Words	0 1
5. C	Key Words	0 1
6. D	Key Words	0 1
Academic Words		
7. D	Academic Words	0 1
8. A	Academic Words	0 1
9. D	Academic Words	0 1
10. B	Academic Words	0 1
11. C	Academic Words	0 1
12. B	Academic Words	0 1
Word Study		
13. D	Word Analysis	0 1
14. C	Word Analysis	0 1
15. A	Word Analysis	0 1
16. B	Word Analysis	0 1
17. D	Word Analysis	0 1

Answer	Tested Skill	Score
Reading		(Circle one.)
18. C	Identify Main Idea	0 1
19. A	Comprehension	0 1
20. D	Identify Cause and Effect	0 1
21. C	Identify Details	0 1
22. B	Identify Details	0 1
23. D	Comprehension	0 1
Grammar		
24. B	Cause and Effect	0 1
25. C	Cause and Effect	0 1
26. A	Cause and Effect	0 1
27. B	Cause and Effect	0 1
28. C	Cause and Effect	0 1
29. D	Cause and Effect	0 1
30. A	Cause and Effect	0 1

_____ ÷ **30** x **100** = _____
(Student's Total Score) (Total Possible Points) (Student's Percent Score)

Unit 1 Unit Test Answer Key and Tested Skills Chart

Answer	Tested Skill	Score
Listening and Reading Comprehension		(Circle one.)
1. C	Listening/Paraphrase	0 1
2. C	Listening/Answer Questions	0 1
3. D	Listening/Answer Questions	0 1
4. A	Listening/Answer Questions	0 1
5. A	Character Motivation	0 1
6. B	Comprehension	0 1
7. B	Identify Cause and Effect	0 1
8. C	Plot	0 1
9. B	Comprehension	0 1
10. B	Answer Questions	0 1
11. A	Comprehension	0 1
12. D	Comprehension	0 1
13. A	Plot/Character Motivation	0 1
14. D	Character Motivation	0 1
15. A	Answer Questions	0 1
16. C	Symbolism	0 1
17. B	Comprehension	0 1
18. D	Answer Questions	0 1
19. B	Comprehension	0 1
20. D	Comprehension	0 1
Vocabulary		
21. D	Key Words	0 1
22. D	Key Words	0 1
23. C	Key Words	0 1
24. C	Key Words	0 1
25. C	Literary Words	0 1
26. B	Literary Words	0 1
27. D	Literary Words	0 1
28. B	Literary Words	0 1
29. C	Academic Words	0 1
30. D	Academic Words	0 1
31. A	Academic Words	0 1
32. C	Academic Words	0 1

Answer	Tested Skill	Score
Word Study		(Circle one.)
33. A	Antonyms	0 1
34. B	Prefixes	0 1
35. D	Prefixes	0 1
36. D	Spelling/Plurals	0 1
37. D	Spelling/Plurals	0 1
38. C	Spelling/Plurals	0 1
39. B	Spelling	0 1
40. D	Spelling	0 1
41. A	Spelling	0 1
42. B	Phonics	0 1
43. D	Phonics	0 1
44. B	Phonics	0 1
Grammar		
45. C	Word Order	0 1
46. A	Word Order	0 1
47. B	Comparison Structures	0 1
48. C	Comparison Structures	0 1
49. C	Parts of Speech	0 1
50. B	Parts of Speech	0 1
51. D	Word Order	0 1
52. A	Comparison Structures	0 1
53. C	Comparison Structures	0 1
54. A	Comparison Structures	0 1
55. C	Subject/Verb Agreement	0 1
Writing		(Score with rubric.)
56-65.	Select a Focus	_____
	Group Related Ideas	
	Write Descriptions	
	Use Descriptive Words	
	Sentence Structure	
	Punctuation and Capitalization	
Oral Reading Fluency		(Circle one.)
66-75.	Speed	0 1 2
	Accuracy	0 1 2
	Expression	0 1 2
	Intonation	0 1 2
	Self-correction	0 1 2

_____ ÷ **75** x **100** = _____
(Student's Total Score) (Total Possible Points) (Student's Percent Score)

Unit 2 Unit Test Answer Key and Tested Skills Chart

Answer	Tested Skill	Score
Listening and Reading Comprehension		(Circle one.)
1. C	Listening/Paraphrase	0 1
2. B	Listening/Paraphrase	0 1
3. A	Listening/Make Inferences	0 1
4. B	Listening/Summarize	0 1
5. A	Plot	0 1
6. B	Character Motivation	0 1
7. A	Plot	0 1
8. A	Symbolism	0 1
9. B	Identify Cause and Effect	0 1
10. A	Identify Cause and Effect	0 1
11. A	Identify Cause and Effect	0 1
12. C	Restate Facts	0 1
13. B	Restate Facts	0 1
14. D	Restate Facts	0 1
15. B	Identify Cause and Effect	0 1
16. C	Restate Facts	0 1
17. C	Character	0 1
18. D	Character	0 1
19. A	Character	0 1
20. D	Setting	0 1
Vocabulary		
21. B	Key Words	0 1
22. C	Key Words	0 1
23. C	Key Words	0 1
24. A	Key Words	0 1
25. A	Literary Words	0 1
26. D	Literary Words	0 1
27. D	Literary Words	0 1
28. C	Literary Words	0 1
29. A	Academic Words	0 1
30. A	Academic Words	0 1
31. C	Academic Words	0 1
32. B	Academic Words	0 1

Answer	Tested Skill	Score
Word Study		(Circle one.)
33. D	Word Roots	0 1
34. C	Word Roots	0 1
35. A	Word Roots	0 1
36. A	Suffixes	0 1
37. C	Suffixes	0 1
38. A	Suffixes	0 1
39. B	Parts of Speech	0 1
40. C	Parts of Speech	0 1
41. D	Parts of Speech	0 1
42. A	Spelling/Plurals	0 1
43. D	Spelling/Plurals	0 1
44. C	Spelling/Inflections	0 1
Grammar		
45. D	Simple Past	0 1
46. B	Simple Past	0 1
47. C	Active and Passive Voice	0 1
48. A	Active and Passive Voice	0 1
49. B	Adjectives	0 1
50. C	Adverb Clause of Time	0 1
51. D	Simple Past	0 1
52. C	Simple Past	0 1
53. A	Adjectives	0 1
54. A	Adverb Clauses of Time	0 1
55. A	Active and Passive Voice	0 1
Writing		(Score with rubric.)
56-65.	Write a Letter	_____
	Select a Focus	
	Include Descriptive Details	
	Sentence Structure	
	Punctuation and Capitalization	
Oral Reading Fluency		(Circle one.)
66-75.	Speed	0 1 2
	Accuracy	0 1 2
	Expression	0 1 2
	Intonation	0 1 2
	Self-correction	0 1 2

_____ ÷ **75** x **100** = _____
(Student's Total Score)   (Total Possible Points)   (Student's Percent Score)

Unit 3 Unit Test Answer Key and Tested Skills Chart

Answer	Tested Skill	Score
Listening and Reading Comprehension		(Circle one.)
1. C	Listening/Summarize	0 1
2. B	Listening/Paraphrase	0 1
3. B	Listening/Paraphrase	0 1
4. D	Listening/Identify Details	0 1
5. C	Answer Questions	0 1
6. A	Identify Main Idea	0 1
7. B	Identify Main Idea	0 1
8. C	Answer Questions	0 1
9. D	Restate Facts	0 1
10. A	Answer Questions	0 1
11. C	Theme/Figurative Language	0 1
12. B	Identify Cause and Effect/ Make Inferences	0 1
13. C	Plot/Identify Cause and Effect	0 1
14. B	Character/Answer Questions	0 1
15. A	Character/Answer Questions	0 1
16. A	Character Motivation/ Identify Cause and Effect	0 1
17. C	Character/Answer Questions	0 1
18. D	Plot	0 1
19. D	Answer Questions	0 1
20. D	Setting	0 1
Vocabulary		
21. D	Key Words	0 1
22. C	Key Words	0 1
23. A	Key Words	0 1
24. B	Key Words	0 1
25. B	Literary Words	0 1
26. A	Literary Words	0 1
27. C	Literary Words	0 1
28. D	Literary Words	0 1
29. A	Academic Words	0 1
30. C	Academic Words	0 1
31. B	Academic Words	0 1
32. D	Academic Words	0 1

Answer	Tested Skill	Score
Word Study		(Circle one.)
33. A	Prefixes	0 1
34. D	Prefixes	0 1
35. C	Prefixes	0 1
36. C	Spelling/Simple Past	0 1
37. B	Spelling/Gerunds	0 1
38. A	Spelling/Simple Past	0 1
39. C	Homophones	0 1
40. A	Homophones	0 1
41. D	Homophones	0 1
42. D	Word Origins	0 1
43. B	Word Origins	0 1
44. C	Word Origins	0 1
Grammar		
45. B	Relative Clauses	0 1
46. D	Gerunds	0 1
47. D	Gerunds	0 1
48. A	Infinitives	0 1
49. B	Impersonal Pronouns	0 1
50. A	Impersonal Pronouns	0 1
51. A	Relative Clauses	0 1
52. B	Relative Clauses	0 1
53. A	Gerunds	0 1
54. A	Infinitives	0 1
55. D	Infinitives	0 1
Writing		(Score with rubric.)
56-65.	Select a Focus	_____
	Use Cause and Effect Structures	
	Write Descriptions	
	Sentence Structure	
	Punctuation and Capitalization	
Oral Reading Fluency		(Circle one.)
66-75.	Speed	0 1 2
	Accuracy	0 1 2
	Expression	0 1 2
	Intonation	0 1 2
	Self-correction	0 1 2

_____ ÷ **75** x **100** = _____
(Student's Total Score) (Total Possible Points) (Student's Percent Score)

Answer	Tested Skill	Score
Listening and Reading Comprehension		(Circle one.)
1. D	Listening/Answer Questions	0 1
2. A	Listening/Answer Questions/Character	0 1
3. B	Listening/Character Motivation	0 1
4. C	Listening/Identify Cause and Effect	0 1
5. B	Make Inferences	0 1
6. A	Identify Main Idea	0 1
7. B	Answer Questions	0 1
8. D	Answer Questions	0 1
9. B	Recognize Sequence	0 1
10. C	Identify Cause and Effect	0 1
11. A	Answer Questions	0 1
12. D	Answer Questions	0 1
13. B	Recognize Sequence/ Setting	0 1
14. A	Answer Questions	0 1
15. D	Identify Cause and Effect/ Character Motivation	0 1
16. D	Identify Cause and Effect	0 1
17. C	Identify Cause and Effect	0 1
18. D	Identify Main Idea/Theme	0 1
19. B	Symbolism	0 1
20. D	Theme/Interpretation	0 1
Vocabulary		
21. D	Key Words	0 1
22. A	Key Words	0 1
23. B	Key Words	0 1
24. A	Key Words	0 1
25. C	Literary Words	0 1
26. A	Literary Words	0 1
27. C	Literary Words	0 1
28. C	Literary Words	0 1
29. A	Academic Words	0 1
30. D	Academic Words	0 1
31. B	Academic Words	0 1
32. A	Academic Words	0 1

Answer	Tested Skill	Score
Word Study		(Circle one.)
33. C	Parts of Speech	0 1
34. A	Parts of Speech	0 1
35. A	Parts of Speech	0 1
36. C	Synonyms	0 1
37. B	Synonyms	0 1
38. A	Synonyms	0 1
39. D	Capitalization	0 1
40. C	Capitalization	0 1
41. C	Capitalization	0 1
42. C	Phonics	0 1
43. D	Phonics	0 1
44. C	Phonics	0 1
Grammar		
45. D	Present Perfect	0 1
46. C	Future with *will*	0 1
47. B	Conjunctions	0 1
48. C	Conjunctions	0 1
49. B	Possessive Adjective	0 1
50. A	Possessive Adjective	0 1
51. A	Present Perfect	0 1
52. B	Conjunctions	0 1
53. A	Future with *will*	0 1
54. D	Future with *will*	0 1
55. A	Conjunctions	0 1
Writing		(Score with rubric.)
56-65.	Select a Focus	_____
	Write a Persuasive Letter	
	Structure	
	Sentence Structure	
	Punctuation and	
	Capitalization	
Oral Reading Fluency		(Circle one.)
66-75.	Speed	0 1 2
	Accuracy	0 1 2
	Expression	0 1 2
	Intonation	0 1 2
	Self-correction	0 1 2

_____ ÷ **75** x **100** = _____
(Student's Total Score)   (Total Possible Points)   (Student's Percent Score)

Answer	Tested Skill	Score
Listening and Reading Comprehension		(Circle one.)
1. A	Listening/Answering Questions	0 1
2. C	Listening/Answering Questions	0 1
3. C	Listening/Paraphrase/ Summarize	0 1
4. D	Listening/Paraphrase/ Summarize	0 1
5. C	Setting	0 1
6. D	Summarize	0 1
7. B	Theme	0 1
8. A	Draw Conclusions/Theme	0 1
9. C	Comprehension	0 1
10. C	Comprehension	0 1
11. B	Comprehension	0 1
12. D	Answer Questions	0 1
13. D	Answer Questions	0 1
14. B	Identify Cause and Effect	0 1
15. C	Answer Questions	0 1
16. C	Comprehension	0 1
17. B	Setting/Plot	0 1
18. A	Plot	0 1
19. A	Character	0 1
20. D	Character	0 1
Vocabulary		
21. D	Key Words	0 1
22. B	Key Words	0 1
23. C	Key Words	0 1
24. D	Key Words	0 1
25. A	Literary Words	0 1
26. C	Literary Words	0 1
27. D	Literary Words	0 1
28. B	Literary Words	0 1
29. B	Academic Words	0 1
30. A	Academic Words	0 1
31. D	Academic Words	0 1
32. C	Academic Words	0 1

Answer	Tested Skill	Score
Word Study		(Circle one.)
33. C	Synonyms	0 1
34. A	Synonyms	0 1
35. B	Synonyms	0 1
36. C	Phonics	0 1
37. A	Phonics	0 1
38. B	Phonics	0 1
39. C	Compound Nouns	0 1
40. B	Compound Nouns	0 1
41. D	Compound Nouns	0 1
42. A	Homophones	0 1
43. A	Homophones	0 1
44. B	Homophones	0 1
Grammar		
45. C	Complex Sentences/ Past Perfect	0 1
46. B	Imperatives	0 1
47. D	Modals	0 1
48. B	Modals	0 1
49. A	Comparison Structure	0 1
50. C	Comparison Structure	0 1
51. D	Independent and Dependent Clauses/ Past Perfect	0 1
52. A	Imperatives	0 1
53. B	Imperatives	0 1
54. A	Modals	0 1
55. A	Comparison Structures	0 1
Writing		(Score with rubric.)
56–65.	Write a Persuasive Letter	_____
	Select a Focus	
	Write a Description	
	Sentence Structure	
	Punctuation and Capitalization	
Oral Reading Fluency		(Circle one.)
66–75.	Speed	0 1 2
	Accuracy	0 1 2
	Expression	0 1 2
	Intonation	0 1 2
	Self-correction	0 1 2

_____	÷	**75**	x	**100**	=	_____	
(Student's Total Score)		(Total Possible Points)				(Student's Percent Score)	

Answer	Tested Skill	Score
Listening and Reading Comprehension		(Circle one.)
1. C	Listening/Summarize	0 1
2. B	Listening/Answer Questions/Point of View	0 1
3. D	Listening/Setting	0 1
4. B	Listening/Answer Questions/Point of View	0 1
5. B	Identify Cause and Effect/ Character Motivation	0 1
6. A	Plot	0 1
7. B	Identify Cause and Effect/ Character Motivation	0 1
8. B	Plot	0 1
9. A	Answer Questions	0 1
10. C	Comprehension	0 1
11. B	Identify Cause and Effect	0 1
12. B	Comprehension	0 1
13. C	Plot /Answer Questions	0 1
14. B	Comprehension	0 1
15. B	Identify Cause and Effect/ Character Motivation	0 1
16. B	Plot /Answer Questions	0 1
17. B	Identify Cause and Effect	0 1
18. B	Restate Facts and Details	0 1
19. A	Answer Questions	0 1
20. B	Identify Details/ Restate Facts and Details	0 1
Vocabulary		
21. D	Key Words	0 1
22. B	Key Words	0 1
23. B	Key Words	0 1
24. B	Key Words	0 1
25. A	Literary Words	0 1
26. D	Key Words	0 1
27. C	Key Words	0 1
28. B	Key Words	0 1
29. C	Academic Words	0 1
30. A	Academic Words	0 1
31. B	Academic Words	0 1
32. B	Academic Words	0 1

Answer	Tested Skill	Score
Word Study		(Circle one.)
33. B	Antonyms	0 1
34. C	Antonyms	0 1
35. B	Antonyms	0 1
36. D	Phonics	0 1
37. C	Phonics	0 1
38. B	Phonics	0 1
39. A	Prefixes and Suffixes	0 1
40. C	Prefixes and Suffixes	0 1
41. B	Prefixes and Suffixes	0 1
42. A	Root W ords	0 1
43. C	Root Words	0 1
44. D	Root Words	0 1
Grammar		
45. B	Modals	0 1
46. A	Adjectives ending in -ing and -ed	0 1
47. B	Adjectives ending in -ing and -ed	0 1
48. A	Quoted Speech	0 1
49. C	Cause and Effect	0 1
50. C	Cause and Effect	0 1
51. A	Modals	0 1
52. D	Adjectives ending in -ing and -ed	0 1
53. D	Quoted Speech	0 1
54. B	Quoted Speech	0 1
55. A	Cause and Effect	0 1
Writing		(Score with rubric.)
56-65.	Understand the Purpose of Reference Materials	_____
	Select a Focus	
	Choose a Format	
	Sentence Structure	
	Punctuation and Capitalization	
Oral Reading Fluency		(Circle one.)
66-75.	Speed	0 1 2
	Accuracy	0 1 2
	Expression	0 1 2
	Intonation	0 1 2
	Self-correction	0 1 2

_____ ÷ **75** x **100** = _____
(Student's Total Score) (Total Possible Points) (Student's Percent Score)

Answer

Taking a Test
1. D
2. C
3. A
4. B
5. B
6. C
7. D
8. C

Answering Questions about a Passage
1. B
2. D
3. D
4. B

Answering Multiple-Choice Questions
1. C
2. B
3. C
4. D

Answering Questions about Meanings of Words
1. D
2. C
3. C
4. A

Answering Fill-in-the-Blank Items
1. A
2. C
3. B
4. A
5. A
6. A

Responding to a Writing Prompt
(Score with rubric on page xii.)

B KEYSTONE

**Diagnostic Pretest,
Midterm Test, and Posttest**

DIAGNOSTIC PRETEST

LISTENING AND READING COMPREHENSION

DIRECTIONS
Listen to the first passage. Choose the best phrase that completes the sentence. Circle the letter of the correct answer. Then listen to the second passage. Choose the best phrase that completes the sentence. Circle the letter of the correct answer.

Passage 1: "Benny's Birthday Blues"

1. The first thing Benny wanted to do at his party was _____.
   - A. to open his presents
   - B. to cut his cake
   - C. to talk and laugh
   - D. to make a list

2. If Benny liked a present he _____.
   - A. passed it around
   - B. said thank you
   - C. jumped up and down
   - D. cut a piece of cake

3. People left the party early because _____.
   - A. it was a school night
   - B. their parents arrived
   - C. they were hungry
   - D. they were bored

4. Benny thought his party would be a success because _____.
   - A. he baked a cake
   - B. he made a plan
   - C. everyone came
   - D. it was Friday

Passage 2: "A Great Idea"

5. Gutenberg's printing press made printing _____.
   - A. less expensive
   - B. more expensive
   - C. more difficult
   - D. less exciting

6. Gutenberg's profession was _____.
   - A. a scientist
   - B. a scholar
   - C. a goldsmith
   - D. a journalist

7. The printing press allowed scientists to _____.
   - A. travel together
   - B. share information
   - C. argue about theories
   - D. write novels

8. Gutenberg probably developed the printing press because he _____.
   - A. was bored with his job
   - B. had a great idea
   - C. needed money
   - D. had a difficult life

GO ON

> ### "Friends are Forever"
>
> Rowena was worried. All of her friends had joined the soccer team. They wanted her to join, too. However, Rowena wasn't interested in soccer.
>
> For her birthday, her father had given her a "dream gift"—a guitar. Now, whenever she had some extra time, she would take the guitar out of its case and practice until her fingers hurt. One day, while Rowena was practicing, her friends came over to her house. "Wow! You play very well!" one friend said.
>
> "I have a great idea," another said, "you can play victory songs for us when we win a soccer game."
>
> Rowena smiled. "I was worried you wouldn't be my friends if I didn't play soccer."
>
> "We would never be so mean."
>
> "Friends are forever."

9. Why was Rowena worried?
   A. She wanted more time to practice her guitar.
   B. Her fingers hurt from practicing guitar too much.
   C. Her friends didn't think she played her guitar well.
   D. Her friends had joined the soccer team but she had not.

10. Why did Rowena's father give her a guitar?
    A. He gave her a guitar during her vacation.
    B. He gave her a guitar for her birthday.
    C. He gave her a guitar in her dreams.
    D. He gave her a guitar for earning good grades.

11. What is Rowena's problem?
    A. She got hurt playing soccer, so she is afraid to join the team.
    B. She wants to play guitar, but her friends want to play soccer.
    C. Her friends broke her guitar while playing soccer.
    D. She wanted a soccer ball, but her father bought her a guitar.

12. How is Rowena's problem solved?
    A. Her friends are happy that she plays guitar.
    B. She finds new friends that like playing guitar.
    C. She sells her guitar and joins the soccer team.
    D. Her friends buy her a soccer ball for her birthday.

GO ON

Leo always asked questions. He asked his teachers, his parents, and his friends. One day, his teacher Ms. Kim gave him a book called *Answers to All Your Questions*. Leo was happy to read the answers to some of his biggest questions.

Leo's Big Questions (with Answers)

1. **Why do camels have humps?** A camel's hump is made of fat. This helps a camel survive in the desert for many days without food.

2. **Why do cats meow?** Usually a cat meows because it wants someone to give it food or let it go outside.

3. **Why do bears hibernate in winter?** Bears sleep through winter because there is not much food available to them.

4. **Why do rats have long tails?** A rat's long tail helps it to balance. Also, the tail helps the body stay at the right temperature.

5. **Why do zebras have stripes?** No one knows this answer for sure, but many scientists believe that a zebra's stripes looks similar to the tall grass where they live. Therefore, the stripes help them hide from predators.

13. What is a camel's hump made of?
    A. It is made of muscle.
    B. It is made of water.
    C. It is made of fat.
    D. It is made of blood.

14. Why do bears hibernate in winter?
    A. because little food is available
    B. to hide from hunters
    C. because snow makes a good cave
    D. because ponds and lakes freeze

15. What do all of Leo's questions have in common?
    A. They are the same length.
    B. They are about animals.
    C. They are difficult to answer.
    D. They are about people with pets.

16. Who answered Leo's questions?
    A. his teacher
    B. Leo
    C. a book
    D. his father

DIRECTIONS

Choose the word or words that best complete each sentence. Circle the letter of the correct answer.

17. The time and place of a story's action is called _____.
    A. stage
    B. setting
    C. history
    D. scene

18. *The golden sun melted into the trees, which swayed with the wind,* is an example of _____.
    A. authentic voice
    B. nature program
    C. sensory detail
    D. first-person point of view

19. A person who takes part in the action of a story is called a _____.
    A. moral
    B. puppet
    C. narrator
    D. character

20. *This tree is a giant. All the other trees are dwarves next to it,* is an example of _____.

    A. analysis
    B. simile
    C. metaphor
    D. identity

21. A group of lines in a poem is called a _____.

    A. bridge
    B. stanza
    C. speech
    D. length

22. *At midnight, he had told them everything would change. Everyone stayed awake to see what would happen,* is an example of _____.
    A. suspense
    B. setting
    C. fortune
    D. sensory detail

23. *Morton Village in 1882 was a dusty, desolate town* is an example of _____.
    A. setting
    B. conflict
    C. personification
    D. characterization

24. A living thing is called a(n) _____.
    A. species
    B. habitat
    C. organism
    D. photosynthesis

25. The air that surrounds the earth is called its _____.
    A. precipitation
    B. evaporation
    C. atmosphere
    D. environment

DIRECTIONS
Choose the word that best completes each sentence. Circle the letter of the correct answer.

26. The officer on a ship or aircraft who plans the route that it travels is called a(n) _____.
    A. navigator
    B. merchant
    C. accountant
    D. prospector

27. Suffering or death caused by not having enough to eat is called _____.
    A. destination
    B. starvation
    C. migration
    D. direction

28. If you did something better than almost everyone else then you _____.
    A. exhibited
    B. acquired
    C. devoted
    D. excelled

29. Someone who designs, builds and repairs roads, bridges, and machines is called a(n) _____.
    A. programmer
    B. physicist
    C. engineer
    D. athlete

30. _____: way from one place to another.
    A. project
    B. route
    C. crate
    D. cycle

31. _____: leave someone or something that you are responsible for.
    A. collapse
    B. abandon
    C. investigate
    D. reconcile

32. _____: as much as one needs; enough.
    A. legitimate
    B. reticent
    C. equivalent
    D. sufficient

33. _____: influence; produce a change.
    A. affect
    B. attain
    C. appeal
    D. attract

GO ON

DIRECTIONS
Read each question below and find the correct answer. Circle the letter of the correct answer.

34. What is the plural form of *monkey*?
    A. monkeys
    B. monkeis
    C. monkeyes
    D. monkees

35. What is the superlative of *scary*?
    A. scarier
    B. scariest
    C. scared
    D. scary

36. Which is the correct inflection of *clap*?
    A. clapping
    B. claping
    C. clap
    D. clapped

37. What is the prefix in the word *invisible*?
    A. able-
    B. invis-
    C. vis-
    D. in-

38. Which of the following is a compound noun?
    A. desert
    B. rattlesnake
    C. reflecting
    D. rattling

39. Which word has the same vowel sound as the underlined part of sp<u>ace</u>?
    A. meet
    B. crude
    C. lake
    D. lapped

40. Which word has the same vowel sound as the underlined part of sli<u>gh</u>t?
    A. lid
    B. stick
    C. knee
    D. by

GO ON

Name _____ Date _____

GRAMMAR

DIRECTIONS
Choose the word or phrase that best completes each sentence. Circle the letter of the correct answer.

41. Last month, they _____ elected to the student council.
    A. was
    B. were
    C. be
    D. went

42. My cousin _____ the package that I sent in December.
    A. got
    B. was got
    C. get
    D. gets

43. What is the sentence *The people elected the President* changed to the passive voice?
    A. The President elected by the people.
    B. The President was elected by the people.
    C. The President were elected by the people.
    D. The President was elect by the people.

44. _____ sleeps as late as possible on weekends.
    A. He
    B. We
    C. They
    D. You

45. Ms. Dant has not seen her pet _____ she left the house this morning.
    A. whenever
    B. since
    C. until
    D. while

46. Degas painted many beautiful pictures _____ were of ballet dancers.
    A. that
    B. who
    C. whom
    D. what

47. He ran five laps around the track _____ his endurance.
    A. to increase
    B. increases
    C. increase
    D. increased

48. The books, pencils, pens, _____ computers are being shipped late.
    A. but
    B. and
    C. or
    D. so

49. A hurricane is _____ than a spring shower.
    A. dangerous
    B. most dangerous
    C. more dangerous
    D. danger

50. *"The plane is just about to land, Tasha said.* A quotation mark is needed _____.

    A. after *land* and before the comma
    B. after *land* and after the comma
    C. after *said* and before the period
    D. after *said* and after the period

Diagnostic Pretest • Grammar

DIRECTIONS

Imagine traveling to a place that is very different from where you live now. Write a letter to a friend and describe this place. Include details that will help your friend picture the place. Write on the lines below.

_____

_____

_____

_____

_____

_____

_____

_____

_____

_____

_____

_____

_____

_____

_____

_____

_____

_____

STOP

ORAL READING FLUENCY SCORE SHEET

Rowena was worried. All of her friends had joined	9
the soccer team. They wanted her to join, too. However,	19
Rowena wasn't interested in soccer.	24
For her birthday, her father had given her a "dream	34
gift"—a guitar! Now, whenever she had some extra time, she	45
would take the guitar out of its case and practice until her	57
fingers hurt. One day, while Rowena was practicing, her	66
friends came over to her house. "Wow! You play very well!" one	78
friend said.	80
"I have a great idea," another said, "you can play victory	91
songs for us when we win a soccer game!"	100
Rowena smiled. "I was worried you wouldn't be my	109
friends if I didn't play soccer."	115
"We would never be so mean!"	121
"Friends are forever."	124

Fluency Skill Assessed	Points Possible	Points Earned
Student reads with speed.	2	
Student reads with accuracy.	2	
Student reads with expression.	2	
Student reads with intonation.	2	
Student self-corrects.	2	

Total Score _____ / 10

Diagnostic Pretest • Oral Reading Fluency

DIRECTIONS

Read the text below aloud for your teacher. Read with speed, accuracy, expression, and intonation.

Rowena was worried. All of her friends had joined the soccer team. They wanted her to join, too. However, Rowena wasn't interested in soccer.

For her birthday, her father had given her a "dream gift"—a guitar! Now, whenever she had some extra time, she would take the guitar out of its case and practice until her fingers hurt. One day, while Rowena was practicing, her friends came over to her house. "Wow! You play very well!" one friend said.

"I have a great idea," another said, "you can play victory songs for us when we win a soccer game!"

Rowena smiled. "I was worried you wouldn't be my friends if I didn't play soccer."

"We would never be so mean!"

"Friends are forever."

MIDTERM TEST

LISTENING AND READING COMPREHENSION

DIRECTIONS

Listen to the first passage. Choose the phrase that best completes each sentence. Circle the letter of the correct answer. Then listen to the second passage. Choose the phrase that best completes each sentence. Circle the letter of the correct answer.

Passage 1: "Javier and Max"

1. When Javier throws a stick, Max _____.
   A. runs away in fear
   B. barks loudly at it
   C. catches it with his teeth
   D. climbs over it quickly

2. Max sleeps outside because _____.
   A. he protects the house
   B. Javier's mom wants him to
   C. he is too big to sleep inside
   D. Javier likes to sleep by himself

3. Max scratches at the window because _____.
   A. he is hungry
   B. it is cold outside
   C. he misses Javier
   D. he caught a spider

4. Javier wants Max to sleep _____.
   A. in his bedroom
   B. under the window
   C. in the kitchen
   D. on his bed

Passage 2: "California's Redwoods"

5. Some redwood trees are as wide as _____.
   A. twenty horses in harness
   B. ten men standing side-by-side
   C. thirty floors in a skyscraper
   D. fifteen cars stacked up

6. To grow well, redwoods need _____.
   A. a dry climate
   B. a hot climate
   C. a wet climate
   D. a cold climate

7. The writer compares the redwoods to _____.
   A. an ocean
   B. skyscrapers
   C. a forest
   D. elevators

8. The most logical conclusion you can draw from this passage is that _____.
   A. redwood trees grow only in California
   B. you should visit California rather than a big city
   C. we manufacturer many products from redwood lumber
   D. California's redwood trees are among the tallest trees on earth

DIRECTIONS

Read each passage. Then choose the best answer for each question. Circle the letter of the correct answer.

"Soft Music"

Ariel's first piano recital was in two days. It was hot, so Ariel opened the window and then returned to practicing. She was nervous and wished that she could play like Leda, an older girl who made playing piano look as easy as walking.

The doorbell rang and Ariel's mother said, "Ariel, someone is here to see you!"

Ariel wondered who it was. Her visitor walked into the room. It was Leda!

"Hi!" Leda said, "I heard you playing."

"How did you hear me?"

"Well, it's pretty loud," Leda said and smiled. Ariel's cheeks turned red.

"It's okay. I used to play like that, too." Leda sat down at the piano bench. "This song should be played softly and lightly. Think of a little baby bird chirping."

Ariel followed Leda's advice and began to play.

"That's much better!" Leda said.

Ariel knew it was and now she wasn't so nervous to play at the recital.

---

9. Ariel wished she could play like Leda. How did Leda make playing piano look?
   A. She made it look quite difficult.
   B. She made it look very simple.
   C. She made it look like a lot of fun.
   D. She made it look like a performance.

10. Why could Leda hear Ariel playing?
   A. They were next door neighbors.
   B. Ariel was playing loudly.
   C. Leda was visiting Ariel.
   D. They were in the same recital.

11. How would you describe Leda?
   A. She is mean.
   B. She is careless.
   C. She is helpful.
   D. She is like a baby bird.

12. In the beginning of the story, how did Ariel feel about playing in her first recital?
   A. uncomfortable
   B. confident
   C. terrified
   D. nervous

GO ON

While Janelle and Mira sat by the river, a small animal hopped past them. "Look at the toad," Mira said. "I think it's a frog," Janelle replied. "Let's go find out." The girls went inside and researched the differences between toads and frogs. Here are the results of their research:

Differences between Frogs and Toads	
Frogs	**Toads**
• have big eyes that stick out • have long, strong, webbed back feet that are used for swimming and jumping • have smooth skin • like a moist environment (near a river, for example) • lay eggs in clusters	• have short back legs that are good for walking • have bumpy skin • like drier climates • have poison glands behind the eyes • lay eggs in long chains.

13. What did frogs use their webbed back feet for?
    A. For laying eggs in clusters.
    B. For walking around rivers.
    C. For swimming and jumping.
    D. For digging holes in swamps.

14. What kind of skin does a toad have?
    A. A toad has smooth skin.
    B. A toad has bumpy skin.
    C. A toad has wet skin.
    D. A toad has thin skin.

15. How are toads and frogs different?
    A. Frogs have eyes but toads do not.
    B. Frogs need water to live and toads do not.
    C. Toads lay eggs but frogs bear live young.
    D. Toads have poison glands but frogs do not.

16. Based on the chart, what was the creature the girls saw?
    A. a toad
    B. a frog
    C. a salamander
    D. a snake

GO ON

DIRECTIONS

Choose the word or words that best complete each sentence. Circle the letter of the correct answer.

17. Descriptive language that creates word pictures for readers is called _____.
    A. sensation
    B. imagery
    C. setting
    D. repetition

18. *The ocean waves whisper a beautiful message* is an example of _____.
    A. extended metaphor
    B. visualization
    C. magnification
    D. personification

19. A sequence of connected events in a story is _____.
    A. role
    B. stanza
    C. plot
    D. stanza

20. *His eyes shined as brightly as stars in a clear night sky* is an example of _____.
    A. simile
    B. repetition
    C. suspense
    D. character motivation

21. *"We will find Muffy! I just know we will. Soon, we'll find her!" Jenny cried,* is an example of _____.
    A. stanza
    B. setting
    C. suspense
    D. extended metaphor

22. A feeling of excitement or curiosity about what is going to happen next in a piece of literature is called _____.
    A. suspense
    B. motive
    C. repetition
    D. characterization

23. *Everyone called Benny's brother the Soccer King. Benny didn't want to be compared to his brother, so he decided to play baseball instead of soccer,* is an example of _____.
    A. character motivation
    B. suspicious motive
    C. negative assumption
    D. extended metaphor

24. Vitamins and minerals that help an organism stay healthy are _____.
    A. nutrients
    B. habitats
    C. species
    D. viruses

25. The process where water turns into water vapor is _____.
    A. condensation
    B. fibrillation
    C. precipitation
    D. evaporation

GO ON

DIRECTIONS
Choose the word that best completes each sentence. Circle the letter of the correct answer.

26. To buy and sell goods and services is to _____.
   A. explore
   B. trade
   C. borrow
   D. donate

27. Scientists who study living things are _____.
   A. geologists
   B. philologists
   C. physicists
   D. biologists

28. Money awarded to pay for students' schooling is a _____.
   A. dealership
   B. commission
   C. scholarship
   D. theory

29. The creation of a new idea, method or invention is _____.
   A. automation
   B. innovation
   C. corporation
   D. methodology

DIRECTIONS
Choose the correct word for each definition below. Circle the letter of the correct answer.

30. _____: eat or use something.
   A. interact
   B. console
   C. consume
   D. survive

31. _____: become larger.
   A. exhale
   B. expand
   C. adjust
   D. aid

32. _____: a promise to do something.
   A. commitment
   B. contribution
   C. fulfillment
   D. priority

33. _____: happening before something else.
   A. primary
   B. previous
   C. global
   D. cultural

GO ON

DIRECTIONS

Read each question below and find the correct answer. Circle the letter of the correct answer.

34. Which language does the word *zero* come from?
    A. Arabic
    B. French
    C. German
    D. Spanish

35. Which is the correct simple past form of *slip*?
    A. slipped
    B. sliped
    C. slip
    D. to slip

36. Which sentence uses the correct homophone?
    A. Krista picked a <u>rows</u>.
    B. <u>Wear</u> are you going?
    C. I have a <u>blue</u> coat.
    D. The dog wagged its <u>tale</u>.

37. Which word can form a new word with the prefix *under-*?
    A. solution
    B. national
    C. billionaire
    D. developed

38. Which word is spelled <u>incorrectly</u>?
    A. begged
    B. rolled
    C. playing
    D. cryeing

39. Which word can form a new word with the prefix *re-*?
    A. note
    B. pay
    C. listen
    D. walk

40. Which word can form a new word with the prefix *re-*?
    A. write
    B. hear
    C. speak
    D. feel

GRAMMAR

DIRECTIONS
Choose the word or words that best complete each sentence. Circle the letter of the correct answer.

41. They live in a _____.
    A. house red brick
    B. brick house red
    C. red brick house
    D. brick red house

42. Which is the gerund in this sentence:
    Reading can help you learn many skills.
    A. reading
    B. can help
    C. you
    D. learn

43. Which is the infinitive in this sentence?
    Her father was surprised to see the gerbil.
    A. her father
    B. was surprised
    C. to see
    D. the gerbil

44. A baseball is _____ a basketball.
    A. so round as
    B. similarly as
    C. as round as
    D. as round that

45. A cat _____ a mouse.
    A. catch
    B. catchs
    C. catchis
    D. catches

46. Which sentence is in the passive voice?
    A. Jane Austen wrote *Emma*.
    B. *Emma* was written by Jane Austen.
    C. They enjoy hiking in the park.
    D. Often, they hike in the park.

47. Which is a dependent clause?
    A. The bank lent money to women
    B. They worked very hard
    C. Herman Schwartz is a professor
    D. Who were very happy in their job

48. Every _____ enjoyed visiting the museum.
    A. student
    B. students
    C. people
    D. visitors

49. What is the sentence *The flowers grow well* changed to the past tense?
    A. The flowers grew well.
    B. The flowers grows well.
    C. The flowers will grow well.
    D. The flowers are growing well.

50. Pamela enjoys _____ the art museum.
    A. visit
    B. to visit
    C. visiting
    D. to visiting

GO ON

DIRECTIONS

Choose someone whom you consider a success: a relative, a friend, a teacher, or a public figure. Write a news article about this person, telling why he or she is a success. In the first paragraph of your article, answer the 5 Ws: *Who? Where? When? What? Why?* Write on the lines below.

_____

_____

_____

_____

_____

_____

_____

_____

_____

_____

_____

_____

_____

_____

_____

_____

_____

_____

ORAL READING FLUENCY SCORE SHEET

Ariel's first piano recital was in two days. It was hot, so	12
Ariel opened the window then returned to practicing. She	21
wished she could play like Leda, an older girl who made	33
playing piano look as easy as walking.	39
The doorbell rang and Ariel's mother shouted, "Ariel,	47
someone is here to see you!"	53
Ariel wondered who it was. Her visitor walked into the room. It	65
was Leda!	67
"Hi!" Leda said, "I heard you playing."	74
"How did you hear me?"	79
"Well, it's pretty loud," Leda said and smiled. Ariel's	89
cheeks turned red.	91
"It's okay. I used to play like that, too." Leda sat down at the	105
piano bench. "This song should be played softly and lightly.	115
Think of a little baby bird chirping."	122
Ariel followed Leda's advice and began to play.	130
"That's much better!"	133
Ariel knew it was and now she wasn't so nervous to play at the	147
recital!	148

Fluency Skill Assessed	Points Possible	Points Earned
Student reads with speed.	2	
Student reads with accuracy.	2	
Student reads with expression.	2	
Student reads with intonation.	2	
Student self-corrects.	2	

Total Score _____ / 10

Midterm Test • Oral Reading Fluency

DIRECTIONS

Read the text below aloud for your teacher. Read with speed, accuracy, expression, and intonation.

Ariel's first piano recital was in two days. It was hot, so Ariel opened the window then returned to practicing. She wished she could play like Leda, an older girl who made playing piano look as easy as walking.

The doorbell rang and Ariel's mother shouted, "Ariel, someone is here to see you!"

Ariel wondered who it was. Her visitor walked into the room. It was Leda!

"Hi!" Leda said, "I heard you playing."

"How did you hear me?"

"Well, it's pretty loud," Leda said and smiled. Ariel's cheeks turned red.

"It's okay. I used to play like that, too." Leda sat down at the piano bench. "This song should be played softly and lightly. Think of a little baby bird chirping."

Ariel followed Leda's advice and began to play.

"That's much better!"

Ariel knew it was and now she wasn't so nervous to play at the recital!

POSTTEST

LISTENING AND READING COMPREHENSION

DIRECTIONS
Listen to the first passage. Choose the best answer for each question. Circle the letter of the correct answer. Then listen to the second passage. Choose the best answer for each question. Circle the letter of the correct answer.

Passage 1: "A Tossed Salad of Words"

1. What kind of word is "Kansas"?
   A. a Nahuatl word
   B. an Iroquois word
   C. a Greek word
   D. a Sioux word

2. What is the reason Rita is writing a letter to Habib?
   A. She hasn't written to him in a long time.
   B. She wants to share what she has learned.
   C. She wants him to memorize new words.
   D. She wants him to move back to Kansas.

3. Why is Rita excited?
   A. She discovered the origin of many words.
   B. She published an interesting magazine article.
   C. She learned what the name of her state means.
   D. She did well on a test about Native Americans.

4. Why does Rita like the fact that words in English come from many different languages?
   A. She wants to learn new languages.
   B. She plans to visit Ohio and Kansas.
   C. She is from a foreign country.
   D. She likes to study the dictionary.

Passage 2: "Lighting up the Dark"

5. Where do many animals that produce their own light live?
   A. in the underbrush of dense rainforests
   B. in small holes in underground caves
   C. in far-back parts of large backyards
   D. in deep parts of the ocean

6. Why are the lights of sea creatures usually a blue-green color?
   A. Blue-green light provides warmth.
   B. Blue-green light keeps predators away.
   C. Blue-green light travels best in water.
   D. Blue-green light sends a positive message.

7. When is having a built-in light most useful?
   A. It is most useful during the day.
   B. It is most useful at school.
   C. It is most useful in summer.
   D. It is most useful at night.

8. What couldn't a laternfish do without a built-in light?
   A. swim
   B. survive
   C. float
   D. sleep

DIRECTIONS
Read each passage. Then choose the best answer for each question. Circle the letter of the correct answer.

"Prepared for Adventure"

Amanda enjoyed hiking with her dad on the weekend. They usually went to Mount Redcliff because it was close to their home. However, this weekend they were hiking up Mount Winslow.

"I can't wait to see the views at the top," Amanda said, pushing up her backpack which had started to slide down.

"You remembered to bring the camera, right?" her father asked.

"Of course! I remembered everything." Amanda always packed items that would help them have a safe hike up the mountain. Amanda had been extra careful this time since they would be hiking in a new place.

After some time had passed, Amanda's dad said, "I'm not sure we're going the right way. Let's look at the map." He studied the map while Amanda used the compass.

"Okay," her father said. "We need to go four miles to the..."

"west!" Amanda finished.

Then they continued on their way.

---

9. When do Amanda and her dad usually hike?
   A. in the summer
   B. on weekdays
   C. at the park
   D. on weekends

10. Who packed safety items for the hike?
    A. Amanda
    B. Amanda's father
    C. Amanda's mother
    D. Amanda's friend

11. What is one reason that Amanda likes to go hiking?
    A. She likes the people she meets.
    B. She likes the wild animals.
    C. She likes the views at the top.
    D. She likes the fresh mountain air.

12. How did Amanda know which way they had to go?
    A. She studied a map.
    B. She used a compass.
    C. She followed the sun.
    D. She saw a trail marker.

GO ON

Posttest • Listening and Reading Comprehension

Maria's class had to write the timeline of a famous person's life. Maria wrote the timeline of the life of Rosa Parks:

February 4, 1913   Rosa Louise McCauley is born in Tuskegee, Alabama.

1932   Rosa marries Raymond Parks, a 29-year old barber.

1945   Rosa Parks registers to vote.

Dec. 1, 1955   Rosa Parks refuses to give up her bus seat to a white man. She is arrested. She becomes widely known because of her courage.

Nov. 3, 1956   The U.S. Supreme Court rules that segregation of buses is unconstitutional.

Aug. 28, 1963   Rosa joins in the March on Washington with Martin Luther King, Jr.

1992   Rosa Parks publishes her first book, *Rosa Parks: My Story.*

1996   Parks receives the Presidential Medal of Freedom.

Oct. 24, 2005   Rosa Parks dies at age 92.

13. Many people learned about Rosa Parks when she _____.
   A. married Raymond Parks, a 29-year old barber
   B. refused to give up her bus seat to a white man
   C. joined the March on Washington
   D. received the Presidential Medal of Freedom

14. Who did Rosa Parks join in the March on Washington?
   A. She joined Raymond Parks.
   B. She joined the President.
   C. She joined Martin Luther King, Jr.
   D. She joined the U.S. Supreme Court.

15. What happened first after Rosa Parks refused to give up her seat?
   A. Rosa Parks died.
   B. She married Raymond Parks.
   C. Bus segregation was ruled unconstitutional.
   D. She received the Presidential Medal of Freedom.

16. People will always remember Rosa Parks _____.
   A. as a courageous woman
   B. as a Supreme Court justice
   C. as the wife of Raymond Parks
   D. as a writer of many books

DIRECTIONS

Choose the word or words that best complete each sentence. Circle the letter of the correct answer.

17. The time and place of a story's action is called _____.
    A. routine
    B. theme
    C. imagery
    D. setting

18. *I followed the wonderful smells until I found the candy shop,* is an example of _____.
    A. self-expression
    B. point-of-view
    C. cross-section
    D. point-of-sale

19. A group of lines in a poem is a _____.
    A. rhyme
    B. simile
    C. ballad
    D. stanza

20. *"Let's ride our bikes to the store,'" Kayla said. Miguel replied, "If we can't walk, I don't want to go." "'Fine, I will go by myself then," Kayla replied,* is an example of _____.
    A. myth
    B. conflict
    C. stage directions
    D. science fiction

21. The central idea, or message, of a work of literature is its _____.
    A. theme
    B. rhyme
    C. scheme
    D. time

22. *Gamil is so fast he can race a tornado and win* is an example of _____.
    A. plot
    B. stage directions
    C. hyperbole
    D. dialogue

23. A fictional story that was told to explain natural events such as wind and rain is a _____.
    A. poetry
    B. hero
    C. myth
    D. epic

24. Plants make food by a process called _____.
    A. reproduction
    B. photosynthesis
    C. decomposition
    D. deduction

25. A group of a particular type of animal that lives together is called a _____.
    A. herd
    B. lichen
    C. calf
    D. tundra

DIRECTIONS
Choose the word or words that best complete each sentence. Circle the letter of the correct answer.

26. Ideas about how something works or why something happens are _____.
    A. designs
    B. methods
    C. theories
    D. robotics

27. Something that is made from a mixture of two or more things is a(n) _____.
    A. hybrid
    B. axis
    C. galaxy
    D. source

28. Working on a farm where cattle, horses or sheep are raised is called _____.
    A. advancing
    B. trampling
    C. advertising
    D. ranching

29. Something moving with a circular movement around a central point is called _____.
    A. formation
    B. rotation
    C. latitude
    D. frustration

DIRECTIONS
Choose the correct word for each of the definitions below. Circle the letter of the correct answer.

30. _____: succeed in doing or gaining something.
    A. occupy
    B. appease
    C. achieve
    D. enforce

31. _____: very close or next to.
    A unspent
    B. blatant
    C. confident
    D. adjacent

32. _____: copy of something that has been slightly changed.
    A. invention
    B. tension
    C. version
    D. vision

33. _____: solid round shape like a ball.
    A. sphere
    B. sphinx
    C. theory
    D. occurrence

GO ON

DIRECTIONS

Read each question below and find the correct answer. Circle the letter of the correct answer.

34. What is the plural of *puppy*?
    A. pupies
    B. puppys
    C. puppies
    D. puppyies

35. Which is the correct simple past form of *log*?
    A. logged
    B. logging
    C. log
    D. logs

36. Which is the prefix in the word *insignificant*?
    A. in-
    B. sign-
    C. fi-
    D. cant

37. Which of the following is a compound noun?
    A. clapped
    B. entered
    C. hugging
    D. eyeglasses

38. Which word is spelled <u>incorrectly</u>?
    A. horrible
    B. visable
    C. terrible
    D. comfortable

39. Which word has the same sound as the underlined part of *tr<u>a</u>ce*?
    A. sleep
    B. food
    C. make
    D. clapped

40. Which word has the same sound as the underlined part of *n<u>igh</u>t*?
    A. skid
    B. brick
    C. ski
    D. sky

GO ON

Name _____ Date _____

GRAMMAR

DIRECTIONS
Choose the word or phrase that best completes each sentence. Circle the letter of the correct answer.

41. A month ago, my family _____ camping.
    A. go
    B. goes
    C. going
    D. went

42. The class _____ a guest speaker last week.
    A. has
    B. had
    C. having
    D. will have

43. The passive voice form of the sentence *Divers discovered a treasure chest* is _____.
    A. Divers were discovered a treasure chest.
    B. A treasure chest were discovered by divers.
    C. A treasure chest was discovered by divers.
    D. By divers was a treasure chest discovered.

44. _____ hears the rooster crow every morning.
    A. She
    B. We
    C. They
    D. I

45. Alysa has not watched television _____ last week.
    A. whenever
    B. since
    C. until
    D. while

46. The salesperson spoke mainly to drivers _____ were interested in car insurance policies.
    A. what
    B. who
    C. whom
    D. which

47. My teacher tried _____ us all.
    A. encouraged
    B. encourage
    C. encouragement
    D. to encourage

48. You can put your coat on the chair, _____ it is better to hang it in the closet.
    A. but
    B. and
    C. or
    D. so

49. Some movie stars are _____ than others.
    A. famous
    B. more famous
    C. most famous
    D. very famous

50. *Liz Greene said, What a beautiful day!"* A quotation mark is needed _____.
    A. after *said* and before the comma
    B. after *said* and after the comma
    C. before *Liz* and after *said*
    D. after *Greene* and after the comma

GO ON

Copyright © by Pearson Education, Inc.

WRITING

DIRECTIONS

Think of three positive ways you have changed in the past two years. Write a letter to a friend who you think may not have noticed these changes. Provide specific examples of how, why, and when you changed. Write on the lines below.

_____

_____

_____

_____

_____

_____

_____

_____

_____

_____

_____

_____

_____

_____

_____

_____

_____

_____

_____

_____

_____

_____

ORAL READING FLUENCY SCORE SHEET

Amanda enjoyed hiking with her dad on the	8
weekend. They usually went to Mount Redcliff because it was	18
close to their home. However, this weekend they were hiking	29
up Mount Winslow.	31
"I can't wait to see the views at the top," Amanda said,	43
pushing up her backpack which had started to slide.	52
"You remembered to bring the camera, right?" her father	61
asked.	62
"Of course! I remembered everything." Amanda always	69
packed items that would help them have a safe hike up the	81
mountain. But Amanda had been extra careful this time since	91
they would be hiking in a new place.	99
After some time had passed, Amanda's dad said, "I'm	109
not sure we're going the right way. Let's look at the map." He	121
studied the map while Amanda used the compass.	129
"Okay," her father said. "We need to go four miles to	140
the…"	141
"West!" Amanda finished.	144
Then they continued on their way.	150

Fluency Skill Assessed	Points Possible	Points Earned
Student reads with speed.	2	
Student reads with accuracy.	2	
Student reads with expression.	2	
Student reads with intonation.	2	
Student self-corrects.	2	

Total Score _____ / 10

Posttest • Oral Reading Fluency

DIRECTIONS
Read the text below aloud for your teacher. Read with speed, accuracy, expression, and intonation.

Amanda enjoyed hiking with her dad on the weekend. They usually went to Mount Redcliff because it was close to their home. However, this weekend they were hiking up Mount Winslow.

"I can't wait to see the views at the top," Amanda said, pushing up her backpack which had started to slide.

"You remembered to bring the camera, right?" her father asked.

"Of course! I remembered everything." Amanda always packed items that would help them have a safe hike up the mountain. But Amanda had been extra careful this time since they would be hiking in a new place.

After some time had passed, Amanda's dad said, "I'm not sure we're going the right way. Let's look at the map." He studied the map while Amanda used the compass.

"Okay," her father said. "We need to go four miles to the…"

"West!" Amanda finished.

Then they continued on their way.

B READING TESTS

READING 1 TEST

LITERARY WORDS

DIRECTIONS
Choose the word or words that best complete each sentence. Circle the letter of the correct answer.

1. Details of sight, sound, smell, taste, or touch are called _____.
   A. literary details
   B. rhyming details
   C. sensory details
   D. imaginary details

2. Descriptive language that creates word pictures for readers is called _____.
   A. imitation
   B. imagery
   C. incentive
   D. imagination

3. The description *soft and wooly* appeals most strongly to the sense of _____.
   A. taste
   B. smell
   C. sound
   D. touch

4. The phrase *whistling winds and claps of thunder* appeals most strongly to the sense of _____.
   A. sight
   B. sound
   C. smell
   D. taste

5. The words *sweet cherries and sour lemons* appeals most strongly to the sense of _____.
   A. smell
   B. sight
   C. touch
   D. taste

6. The phrase *sparkling blue ocean* appeals most strongly to the sense of _____.
   A. sight
   B. taste
   C. smell
   D. touch

GO ON ▶

DIRECTIONS

Choose the correct word for each definition below. Circle the letter of the correct answer.

7. _____: an amount out of every hundred.
   A. cycle
   B. pupae
   C. project
   D. percent

8. _____: sudden and noticeable.
   A. wispy
   B. sticky
   C. freezing
   D. dramatic

9. _____: a plan to do something.
   A. cycle
   B. project
   C. percent
   D. embroidery

10. _____: a set of events that happen again and again.
    A. pupae
    B. cycle
    C. project
    D. percent

WORD STUDY

DIRECTIONS

Choose the best answer for each item. Circle the letter of the correct answer.

11. The word *accurate* means "correct." Which word means "not correct"?
    A. inaccurate
    B. reaccurate
    C. unaccurate
    D. overaccurate

12. The word *heat* means "to make warm." Which word means "to make warm again"?
    A. unheat
    B. inheat
    C. reheat
    D. overheat

13. The word *active* means "lively." Which word means "too lively"?
    A. reactive
    B. unactive
    C. inactive
    D. overactive

14. The word *able* means "capable." Which word means "not capable"?
    A. inable
    B. unable
    C. reable
    D. overable

15. The word *do* means "to complete or perform." Which word means "to complete or perform again"?
    A. redo
    B. undo
    C. indo
    D. overdo

16. The word *pleasant* means "nice." Which word means "not nice"?
    A. inpleasant
    B. repleasant
    C. unpleasant
    D. overpleasant

GO ON

READING: From *Project Mulberry*

DIRECTIONS
Choose the word or phrase that best completes each item or answers each question. Circle the letter of the correct answer.

17. The caterpillar moves its head constantly to _____.
    A. make silk threads
    B. avoid being filmed
    C. find enough leaves
    D. get away from the twins

18. Julia plans to make her cocoon for the project by _____.
    A. drawing a picture with crayons
    B. embroidering it with silk thread
    C. making a display of photographs
    D. gluing layers of cotton like clouds

19. The lifecycle of a silkworm has the following four stages from first to last: _____.
    A. worm, moth, egg, cocoon
    B. egg, worm, cocoon, moth
    C. egg, cocoon, worm, moth
    D. moth, cocoon, egg, worm

20. Patrick says that there will be no moths at the end of their project because _____.
    A. he plans to set all the moths free
    B. the moths will turn into butterflies
    C. the moths will fly away after hatching
    D. the pupae (worms) will die when the cocoons are boiled

21. Why is Julia is very confused about the worms?
    A. She forgot to read the book at all.
    B. She did not understand the book.
    C. She did not finish reading the book.
    D. She forgot how long it takes pupae to hatch.

22. The author shows Julia's feelings by _____.
    A. having her jump up and down
    B. telling about her anger and rage
    C. having Patrick explain her sadness
    D. describing her hands as freezing cold

23. Silk thread is made by _____.
    A. leaving a cocoon on a table
    B. placing a cocoon in boiling water
    C. placing a cocoon in a special cage
    D. placing a cocoon in a sewing machine

GO ON

DIRECTIONS

Choose the words that best complete each sentence. Circle the letter of the correct answer.

24. They live in a _____.
    A. house red brick
    B. brick house red
    C. red brick house
    D. house brick red

25. The sky is a _____.
    A. beautiful blue color
    B. color beautiful blue
    C. blue beautiful color
    D. blue color beautiful

26. I like that _____ vase.
    A. green interesting glass
    B. interesting green glass
    C. glass green interesting
    D. glass interesting green

27. We bought a _____ table.
    A. plastic red large
    B. red plastic large
    C. plastic large red
    D. large red plastic

28. What is in this _____ box?
    A. pretty tiny gold
    B. tiny gold pretty
    C. gold tiny pretty
    D. gold pretty tiny

29. Let's walk across the _____ bridge.
    A. huge steel famous
    B. steel famous huge
    C. famous huge steel
    D. steel huge famous

30. This is my _____ bag.
    A. silk little blue
    B. silk blue little
    C. blue silk little
    D. little blue silk

STOP

Name _____   Date _____

READING 2 TEST

UNIT 1

KEY WORDS

DIRECTIONS
Choose the word or words that best complete each sentence. Circle the letter of the correct answer.

1. Plants make food using sunlight by a process called _____.
   A. nutrients
   B. species
   C. photography
   D. photosynthesis

2. Air, water, and rocks, are examples of _____.
   A. species
   B. organisms
   C. living things
   D. nonliving things

3. Because it is alive, a cat is an example of an _____.
   A. organism
   B. ecosystem
   C. ornament
   D. element

4. When dogs have puppies, they _____.
   A. retrieve
   B. represent
   C. reproduce
   D. decompose

5. Animals that can have babies together belong to the same _____.
   A. enterprise
   B. ecosystem
   C. species
   D. organism

6. In order to grow, plants need _____.
   A. nutrients
   B. organisms
   C. species
   D. populations

GO ON

DIRECTIONS

Choose the correct word for each definition below. Circle the letter of the correct answer.

7. _____: eat or use something.
   A. prefer
   B. produce
   C. consume
   D. interact

8. _____: almost the same, but not exactly the same.
   A. identical
   B. different
   C. familiar
   D. similar

9. _____: have an effect on each other.
   A. interact
   B. consume
   C. movement
   D. compensate

10. _____: the world of land, sea, and air that we live in.
    A. shelter
    B. refuge
    C. environment
    D. background

11. _____: continue to live.
    A. perish
    B. survive
    C. interact
    D. introduce

DIRECTIONS

Read each sentence below. Circle the letter of the sentence with the underlined word that is spelled incorrectly.

12. A. Chicago and Dallas are <u>cities</u>.
    B. The kids are playing with <u>toyes</u>.
    C. There are many tall <u>buildings</u>.
    D. We have two dogs and three <u>cats</u>.

13. A. I am taking six <u>classes</u>.
    B. Animals live in different <u>habitats</u>.
    C. Look at all the <u>houses</u>!
    D. There are different kinds of <u>communityes</u>.

14. A. The <u>boys</u> and girls are here.
    B. Red <u>foxs</u> live in the forest.
    C. We can see <u>whales</u> in Hawaii.
    D. The <u>snakes</u> live in the grass.

15. A. I can't see the <u>animals</u>.
    B. We learned about <u>food chains</u>.
    C. <u>Plants</u> produce oxygen.
    D. Here are three <u>babys</u>.

16. A. I bought paint and <u>brushs</u>.
    B. <u>Carnivores</u> eat meat.
    C. Brazil has many rain <u>forests</u>.
    D. <u>Horses</u> eat mostly grass.

17. A. There are many <u>virusses</u>.
    B. <u>Spiders</u> live all around us.
    C. The <u>monkeys</u> are over there.
    D. <u>Butterflies</u> like warm weather.

GO ON

Name _____ Date _____

DIRECTIONS
Choose the word or phrase that best completes each item or answers each question. Circle the letter of the correct answer.

18. A redwood tree, a mouse, and an insect are all _____.
    A. herbivores
    B. organisms
    C. carnivores
    D. viruses

19. A habitat provides _____ for living things.
    A. different requirements for survival
    B. water, including an ocean, a forest, and a river
    C. different places so they do not get bored
    D. food and water

20. A community includes _____.
    A. all the members of the same species
    B. types of cactus that live in the desert
    C. all the nonliving things in an ecosystem
    D. all the different populations that live in one area

21. All the living and nonliving things in an area make up a(n) _____.
    A. ecosystem
    B. population
    C. organism
    D. species

22. The three main kinds of organisms in an ecosystem are _____.
    A. living, nonliving, and bacteria
    B. populations, scavengers, and habitats
    C. species, consumers, and communities
    D. producers, consumers, and decomposers

23. An animal that eats only plants is called a(n) _____.
    A. carnivore
    B. herbivore
    C. omnivore
    D. scavenger

24. A food chain always begins with a _____.
    A. plant
    B. mouse
    C. consumer
    D. population

GRAMMAR

DIRECTIONS
Choose the word or words that best complete each sentence. Circle the letter of the correct answer.

25. My brother and I are _____ we often fight.
    A. as different as
    B. so similar as
    C. so important that
    D. so different that

26. Monarch butterflies travel from one place to another. _____, some species of whales travel around many oceans.
    A. And
    B. Similarly
    C. Samely
    D. Therefore

27. Nonliving things are _____ living things in an ecosystem.
    A. so similar that
    B. as small as
    C. as necessary as
    D. so important that

28. Consumers are _____ producers.
    A. as green as
    B. as important as
    C. so large that
    D. so common that

29. A whale can grow to be _____ a house.
    A. as large as
    B. so large that
    C. as important as
    D. so numerous that

30. Without water, plants die. _____, without plants, animals cannot live.
    A. After
    B. Similarly
    C. In case
    D. Because

UNIT 1 READING 3 TEST

LITERARY WORDS

DIRECTIONS
Choose the word or words that best complete each sentence. Circle the letter of the correct answer.

1. Writing that creates vivid images and is not meant to be read as fact is called _____.
   A. realistic language
   B. figurative language
   C. fantastical language
   D. exaggerated language

2. The time and place of a story's action is called the _____.
   A. culture
   B. location
   C. setting
   D. geography

3. Giving human qualities to nonhuman things is called _____.
   A. personality
   B. personification
   C. transference
   D. figurative language

4. *The sun is rising on a little farm in Nebraska* is an example of a story's _____.
   A. climate
   B. climax
   C. setting
   D. characters

5. *The wind sighed in the trees* is an example of a type of figurative language called _____.
   A. setting
   B. semester
   C. periscope
   D. personification

GO ON

DIRECTIONS

Choose the correct word for each definition below. Circle the letter of the correct answer.

6. _____: a way from one place to another.
   A. rook
   B. route
   C. ruby
   D. routine

7. _____: able to do something.
   A. gifted
   B. patriotic
   C. discreet
   D. capable

8. _____: change something so that it is suitable for a new situation.
   A. rely
   B. depend
   C. adapt
   D. destroy

9. _____: made a decision based on evidence.
   A. described
   B. concluded
   C. avoided
   D. accomplished

10. _____: trust someone or something.
    A. rely
    B. adapt
    C. adore
    D. promise

DIRECTIONS

Read each item below. Circle the letter of the word or words that are spelled <u>incorrectly</u>.

11. A. grandmother
    B. thirty-three
    C. highschool
    D. Monday

12. A. apple juice
    B. ladybug
    C. sunset
    D. rattle snake

13. A. ninety-nine
    B. vicepresident
    C. overcoat
    D. sunglasses

14. A. soninlaw
    B. underline
    C. brand name
    D. park bench

15. A. eyelash
    B. mother-in-law
    C. wellbeing
    D. toothpaste

16. A. wind-mill
    B. firewood
    C. campfire
    D. twenty-nine

GO ON

READING: "Ali, Child of the Desert" / "Desert Women"

DIRECTIONS
Choose the word or phrase that best answers each question. Circle the letter of the correct answer.

17. At the beginning of the story "Ali, Child of the Desert," Ali and his father are _____.
    A. taking a nap
    B. having lunch
    C. walking across the Sahara Desert
    D. riding their camels

18. During the sandstorm, Ali stays safe by hiding _____.
    A. in a small tent
    B. in a small cave
    C. against his camel
    D. next to his father

19. Which sentence best describes Abdul's dwelling?
    A. It is a one-room adobe hut.
    B. It is a pile of rugs against a tree.
    C. It is a large tent with a wood floor.
    D. It is a palm roof held up by four sticks.

20. Why does Ali decide not to go with Abdul to the mountains?
    A. His camel has gotten hurt.
    B. He likes living in Abdul's dwelling.
    C. He remembers his father's words.
    D. He is afraid of bandits in the mountains.

21. Abdul leaves _____ for Ali and Jabad.
    A. his radio
    B. some dates
    C. his heavy rugs
    D. a goat

22. In the poem "Desert Women," desert women are compared to _____.
    A. songs
    B. breezes
    C. flowers
    D. cactuses

23. The poem describes desert women as _____.
    A. lonely and tired
    B. wealthy and powerful
    C. hungry and thirsty
    D. strong and beautiful

DIRECTIONS
Choose the word or words that correctly complete each sentence. Circle the letter of the correct answer.

24. In the sentence *Help me!* the subject is
_____.
   A. us
   B. you
   C. me
   D. help

25. In the sentence *She walks home from school*, the verb is _____.
   A. she
   B. home
   C. walks
   D. school

26. In the sentence *Ravi sings very well, and he plays the piano*, the conjunction is _____.
   A. and
   B. well
   C. plays
   D. sings

27. In the sentence *Flowers grow in summer*, the predicate is _____.
   A. flowers
   B. grow
   C. in summer
   D. grow in summer

28. In the sentence *Birds chirp in the summer sun*, the subject is _____.
   A. chirp
   B. birds
   C. sun
   D. summer

29. In the sentence *The wind is blowing, but very gently*, the conjunction is _____.
   A. wind
   B. very
   C. gently
   D. but

30. In the sentence *The desert is hot and dry*, the verb is _____.
   A. the
   B. is
   C. hot
   D. and

Name _____ Date _____

KEY WORDS

DIRECTIONS
Choose the word or words that best complete each sentence. Circle the letter of the correct answer.

1. When water evaporates and changes into gas, water _____ forms.
   A. cycle
   B. canal
   C. vapor
   D. version

2. Evaporation, condensation, and precipitation are all part of the _____.
   A. water table
   B. rain gauge
   C. rain date
   D. water cycle

3. Rain, snow, sleet, and hail are all _____.
   A. isolation
   B. perforation
   C. precipitation
   D. condensation

4. Water turns into a gas that rises in the air through a process called _____.
   A. evaporation
   B. exasperation
   C. condensation
   D. precipitation

5. The gases surrounding Earth are the _____.
   A. vapor
   B. equator
   C. universe
   D. atmosphere

6. The process in which water vapor cools and changes into drops of liquid water is called _____.
   A. evaporation
   B. condensation
   C. dispensation
   D. evacuation

GO ON

DIRECTIONS

Choose the correct word for each definition below. Circle the letter of the correct answer.

DIRECTIONS

Choose the word with the same sound as the underlined part of the word in the box. Circle the letter of the correct answer.

7. _____: series of actions.
   A. source
   B. percent
   C. serial
   D. process

8. _____: person, place, or thing that something comes from.
   A. hangar
   B. source
   C. supply
   D. habitat

9. _____: change something so that it is the opposite of what it was before.
   A. review
   B. reverse
   C. renew
   D. react

10. _____: make something new.
    A. consist
    B. check
    C. create
    D. complete

11. _____: able to be used or seen.
    A. available
    B. inadequate
    C. essential
    D. important

12. _____: be made up of.
    A. create
    B. cover
    C. crease
    D. consist

13. fake
    A. track
    B. raise
    C. star
    D. total

14. stay
    A. back
    B. square
    C. camel
    D. afraid

15. strain
    A. hospital
    B. make
    C. lack
    D. harbor

16. wait
    A. rack
    B. airport
    C. Monday
    D. apple

17. trace
    A. army
    B. guitar
    C. race
    D. jar

18. bay
    A. stack
    B. chart
    C. fact
    D. grape

Name _____ Date _____

DIRECTIONS
Choose the word or phrase that best completes each item or answers each question. Circle the letter of the correct answer.

19. Earth's surface and people are alike because both _____.
    A. produce a lot of carbon dioxide
    B. create the water cycle
    C. need salt water to survive
    D. are made mostly of water

20. Only about _____ percent of Earth's water is available for people to use.
    A. 1
    B. 25
    C. 50
    D. 97

21. Groundwater is found mainly _____.
    A. in the North and South Poles
    B. in the Atlantic Ocean
    C. in lakes and streams
    D. between soil and rocks

22. The source of energy that creates the water cycle is the _____.
    A. sun
    B. earth
    C. moon
    D. wind

23. When water vapor cools, it _____.
    A. heats up in the sky
    B. changes into rays of sunlight
    C. condenses into liquid water drops
    D. changes the shape of the clouds

24. One cause of the polluted air and rivers in China is _____.
    A. rapid industrial growth
    B. more and more animals
    C. old-fashioned ways of farming
    D. too many villages in the country

25. People against the South-North Water Diversion Plan say it will _____.
    A. increase water pollution
    B. cause the land to get dry
    C. cause people to move to the area
    D. make the Yellow River too large

GO ON

GRAMMAR

DIRECTIONS
Choose the word that correctly completes each sentence. Circle the letter of the correct answer.

26. The sun _____ in the west.
    A. setting
    B. setted
    C. to set
    D. sets

27. I _____ green apples.
    A. like
    B. likes
    C. lik
    D. liking

28. Plants _____ sun to live.
    A. needs
    B. need
    C. needing
    D. ned

29. We _____ the museum on Tuesdays.
    A. visitt
    B. visiting
    C. visit
    D. visits

30. They _____ a vacation every year.
    A. takes
    B. take
    C. tooks
    D. taked

UNIT 2 READING 1 TEST

LITERARY WORDS

DIRECTIONS
Choose the word or words that best complete each sentence. Circle the letter of the correct answer.

1. A sequence of connected events in a story is called a _____.
   A. plot
   B. thread
   C. narrator
   D. point of view

2. A person who takes part in the action of a story is called a _____.
   A. hero
   B. reader
   C. plot
   D. character

3. When a character tells the story, the writer uses the first-person _____.
   A. pen
   B. plot
   C. opinion
   D. point of view

4. *A search for a treasure chest hidden in a far-away island* is an example of _____.
   A. plot
   B. action
   C. point of view
   D. character

5. *There is an apple tree in front of my house* is an example of _____.
   A. third-person point of view
   B. praise
   C. character
   D. first-person point of view

6. *Ravi, a kind young man in his early twenties* is an example of _____.
   A. plot
   B. preface
   C. character
   D. contraction

GO ON

ACADEMIC WORDS

DIRECTIONS
Choose the correct word for each definition below. Circle the letter of the correct answer.

7. _____: after a long time.
   A. finally
   B. barely
   C. certainly
   D. hopefully

8. _____: behave in a certain way because of what someone has done or said to you.
   A. react
   B. subside
   C. abandon
   D. collapse

9. _____: set of plans and skills to gain success.
   A. task
   B. strategy
   C. structure
   D. assignment

10. _____: fall down suddenly.
    A. falter
    B. abandon
    C. stagger
    D. collapse

11. _____: leave someone or something that you are responsible for.
    A. absorb
    B. investigate
    C. conceal
    D. abandon

12. _____: search for information by looking or asking questions.
    A. collate
    B. activate
    C. recite
    D. investigate

WORD STUDY

DIRECTIONS
Read each question below and find the correct answer. Circle the letter of the correct answer.

13. The root *vict* means "conquer." Which word means "the winner in a battle"?
    A. victor
    B. visa
    C. victim
    D. visitor

14. The root *vis* means "see." Which word means "to form a mental picture"?
    A. visit
    B. view
    C. revise
    D. visualize

15. Which root, when added to the letters *ento*, makes a word meaning "an object that reminds you of the past"?
    A. *vict*
    B. *vis*
    C. *mem*
    D. *laps*

16. Which root, when added to the letters *ate*, makes a word meaning "an official order to do something"?
    A. *mem*
    B. *mand*
    C. *vict*
    D. *laps*

GO ON

Name _____ Date _____

DIRECTIONS
Choose the word or phrase that best completes each item or answers each question. Circle the letter of the correct answer.

17. The gods and goddesses of ancient Greece lived _____.
   A. in the ocean
   B. in a city called Troy
   C. in a leafy green cove
   D. on Mount Olympus

18. Odysseus thinks the Greek warriors had offended _____.
   A. Troy
   B. Zeus
   C. Athena
   D. Poseidon

19. According to Odysseus, Zeus is _____.
   A. hurling thunderbolts at them
   B. offering them beautiful flowers
   C. sending them on a long journey
   D. making them forget the past

20. During the storms, Odysseus ordered his men to _____.
   A. row to shore
   B. jump off the ship
   C. surrender to the storm
   D. hide in the bottom of the ship

21. The islanders are _____.
   A. hostile
   B. friendly
   C. neutral
   D. annoyed

22. Odysseus refuses to eat a lotus flower because _____.
   A. he doesn't think he will like the taste
   B. he doesn't want to offend the islanders
   C. he doesn't want to offend the gods
   D. he doesn't want to forget the past

23. The power of the lotus flowers is best described as _____.
   A. common
   B. magical
   C. nutritious
   D. deadly

DIRECTIONS

Choose the past tense form of the verb that best completes each sentence. Circle the letter of the correct answer.

24. Rachel _____ the topics she had studied would be on the test.
    A. hope
    B. hoped
    C. hopped
    D. hoptp

25. After training for weeks, the runner _____ in great shape.
    A. be
    B. am
    C. was
    D. were

26. Yesterday, I _____ chapter one.
    A. reed
    B. read
    C. red
    D. rode

27. Chan _____ until noon last Saturday.
    A. sleeped
    B. sleepd
    C. slept
    D. sleept

28. The plant _____ three inches!
    A. grew
    B. growed
    C. growd
    D. grewed

29. When I _____ home, the door was locked.
    A. get
    B. getted
    C. gott
    D. got

30. He _____ sick after eating too much candy.
    A. feeled
    B. felt
    C. feeld
    D. fault

READING 2 TEST

KEY WORDS

DIRECTIONS

Choose the word that best completes each sentence. Circle the letter of the correct answer.

1. Societies that are well-organized with large cities are called _____.
   A. markets
   B. colonies
   C. expeditions
   D. civilizations

2. The person who is trained to figure out the path of a ship or aircraft is the _____.
   A. tracker
   B. trader
   C. navigator
   D. namesake

3. Long journeys by a group of people to explore a region are called _____.
   A. routes
   B. markets
   C. experiences
   D. expeditions

4. Open places or buildings with stalls where goods are sold are called _____.
   A. regions
   B. markets
   C. vessels
   D. merchants

5. To exchange one thing for another is to _____.
   A. trade
   B. trace
   C. trail
   D. trample

6. To travel to a new place that is not well-known to find out more about it is an _____.
   A. explosion
   B. exposure
   C. exploration
   D. expression

GO ON

DIRECTIONS

Choose the correct word for each definition below. Circle the letter of the correct answer.

7. _____: large area.
   A. route
   B. rudder
   C. region
   D. restriction

8. _____: gave money for something.
   A. mixed
   B. financed
   C. borrowed
   D. varied

9. _____: led or guided.
   A. traded
   B. restored
   C. ceased
   D. conducted

10. _____: consisting of many different kinds of things.
    A. evolved
    B. ceased
    C. varied
    D. confused

11. _____: started something new.
    A. varied
    B. changed
    C. assembled
    D. established

DIRECTIONS

Choose the correct noun form of each verb in bold type. Circle the letter of the correct answer.

12. **to dance**
    A. a dancer
    B. a danceer
    C. a dancor
    D. a danccer

13. **to create**
    A. a creater
    B. a creator
    C. a creatter
    D. a creattor

14. **to run**
    A. a runer
    B. a runnor
    C. a runner
    D. a runor

15. **to inspect**
    A. an inspecter
    B. an inspecttor
    C. an inspectter
    D. an inspector

16. **to navigate**
    A. a naviogator
    B. a navigator
    C. a navigattor
    D. a navigater

Name _____ Date _____

DIRECTIONS

Choose the word or phrase that best completes each item or answers each question. Circle the letter of the correct answer.

17. The Phoenicians explored _____.
    A. the sea route to the East Indies
    B. the land route between Europe and Asia
    C. the Cape of Good Hope around Africa
    D. the land that bordered the Mediterranean Sea

18. The Phoenicians went to new lands to _____.
    A. capture slaves
    B. buy and sell silk
    C. make money by trading
    D. show off their beautiful ships

19. The Vikings lived in _____.
    A. Britain
    B. Scandinavia
    C. Eastern Europe
    D. the Mediterranean

20. Many Vikings set out to explore new places to _____.
    A. find a new overland route to the East Indies
    B. steal treasures and settle on new farm land
    C. trade horses and gold for silk and spices
    D. learn the secret of making silk

21. Marco Polo came from _____.
    A. Venice, Italy
    B. London, England
    C. the Spice Islands
    D. the southern tip of Africa

22. Prince Henry's ships explored _____.
    A. the North and South Poles
    B. the west coast of Africa
    C. the great deserts of Asia
    D. the west coast of North America

23. Christopher Columbus intended to sail to _____.
    A. Africa
    B. the Caribbean Sea
    C. Spain and Portugal
    D. the East Indies

GRAMMAR

DIRECTIONS

Choose the passive voice form of each sentence. Circle the letter of the correct answer.

24. The dog chased the cat.
    A. The dog chasing the cat.
    B. The cat chased the dog.
    C. The cat was chased by the dog.
    D. The cat were chased at the dog.

25. Cesar read the introduction.
    A. The introduction were read for Cesar.
    B. Cesar was read the introduction.
    C. The introduction was read by Cesar.
    D. The introduction of Cesar was read.

26. The postal worker delivered the mail.
    A. The mail delivered by the postal worker.
    B. The postal worker were delivered the mail.
    C. The mail was delivering the postal worker.
    D. The mail was delivered by the postal worker.

27. My mother scolded me.
    A. Me, I was being scolded by my mother.
    B. I was scolded by my mother.
    C. My mother was scolded me.
    D. I was scolded my mother.

28. People bought spices and gold at the market.
    A. Spices and gold were bought at the market.
    B. At the market, spices and gold were being bought.
    C. By people at the market, spices and gold were being bought.
    D. Spices and gold by people were being bought at the market.

29. Yoko's friends surprised her.
    A. Her friends were surprised for Yoko.
    B. Yoko surprised her friends.
    C. Yoko was surprised by her friends.
    D. Her friends by Yoko were surprised.

30. Explorers discovered exciting new things.
    A. Exciting by explorers new things were discovered.
    B. By explorers, exciting new things were discovered
    C. New things were discovered by exciting explorers.
    D. Exciting new things were discovered by explorers.

READING 3 TEST

KEY WORDS

DIRECTIONS
Choose the word that best completes each sentence. Circle the letter of the correct answer.

1. Scientists who study animals to learn about their lives and behavior are _____.
    A. flutists
    B. geologists
    C. biologists
    D. economists

2. Something that has the power to attract iron or steel is _____.
    A. magnetic
    B. prophetic
    C. majestic
    D. frenetic

3. Suffering or death that is caused by not having enough to eat is _____.
    A. destination
    B. starvation
    C. reservation
    D. donation

4. A group of a particular type of animal that lives together is a _____.
    A. fern
    B. herd
    C. brim
    D. herb

5. A view across an area of land is called a _____.
    A. backcloth
    B. sand dune
    C. seascape
    D. landscape

6. A long trip from one place to another that is usually over a long distance is a _____.
    A. journal
    B. journey
    C. destination
    D. determination

GO ON

DIRECTIONS
Choose the correct word for each definition below. Circle the letter of the correct answer.

7. _____: as much as one needs; enough.
   A. deficient
   B. proficient
   C. sufficient
   D. omniscient

8. _____: moves closer.
   A. ascends
   B. relocates
   C. treads
   D. approaches

9. _____: move or carry goods from one place to another.
   A. transport
   B. degenerate
   C. translate
   D. delegate

10. _____: move from one place to another.
    A. migraine
    B. situate
    C. facilitate
    D. migrate

DIRECTIONS
Read each sentence below. Identify the part of speech of each underlined word. Circle the letter of the correct answer.

11. We have a <u>shoe</u> store in the neighborhood.
    A. noun
    B. adjective
    C. verb
    D. pronoun

12. We went to <u>summer</u> camp this year.
    A. adjective
    B. noun
    C. verb
    D. conjunction

13. The spring <u>rain</u> helps the flowers grow.
    A. verb
    B. noun
    C. adjective
    D. adverb

14. The <u>math</u> lesson is very interesting.
    A. noun
    B. verb
    C. pronoun
    D. adjective

15. The <u>movie</u> poster is beautiful.
    A. pronoun
    B. noun
    C. adjective
    D. verb

16. The <u>restaurant</u> menu is so long!
    A. adjective
    B. noun
    C. verb
    D. conjunction

GO ON

READING: "Migrating Caribou" / "Magnets in Animals"

DIRECTIONS
Choose the word or phrase that best completes each item or answers each question. Circle the letter of the correct answer.

"Migrating Caribou"

17. The Arctic tundra is located _____.
    A. next to the rain forests of South America, close to Brazil
    B. near the dry, rocky, and isolated deserts of Asia and northern Africa
    C. in the cold, treeless regions of northern Asia, Europe, and North America
    D. in the icy, snowy regions of the southern hemisphere, near the South Pole

18. The barren-ground caribou move south because they want _____.
    A. to find a mate
    B. to return home
    C. to avoid starvation
    D. more space to run around

19. Barren-ground caribou most like to eat _____.
    A. lichen
    B. worms
    C. small animals
    D. nuts and berries

20. The caribou go back to the northern Arctic to have their babies because _____.
    A. it is safer there
    B. it is prettier there
    C. it is much warmer there
    D. there are fewer animals there

21. The caribou travel _____.
    A. in pairs
    B. on their own
    C. in large herds
    D. with wolves and bears

"Magnets in Animals"

22. Monarch butterflies spend the winter in _____.
    A. Mexico
    B. Canada
    C. the open sea
    D. the northern United States

23. Some migrating animals find their way because they _____.
    A. have a built-in compass
    B. go in the direction the wind blows
    C. travel very slowly and carefully
    D. have traveled the same roads for years

GO ON

DIRECTIONS
Choose the word that best completes each sentence. Circle the letter of the correct answer.

24. There is something _____ about a sunrise.
    A. forgivable
    B. inspiring
    C. successful
    D. studious

25. It is _____ to say, "Please, excuse me."
    A. polite
    B. rude
    C. casual
    D. rough

26. There is nothing _____ with asking a question.
    A. warm
    B. blunt
    C. older
    D. wrong

27. Anna brushes her _____ hair.
    A. suspicious
    B. lucky
    C. shiny
    D. ready

28. The _____ dog barked at the stranger.
    A. exact
    B. fierce
    C. rigid
    D. fresh

29. Can you think of someplace _____ we can visit?
    A. special
    B. polite
    C. vague
    D. rusty

30. Henri wore blue _____ pants to school.
    A. positive
    B. younger
    C. gloomy
    D. denim

STOP

Unit 2 • Reading 3 Test Grammar

READING 4 TEST

LITERARY WORDS

DIRECTIONS
Choose the word that best completes each sentence. Circle the letter of the correct answer.

1. A figure of speech that writers use to make a comparison between two different things is a _____.
   A. rhyme
   B. metaphor
   C. reversal
   D. metronome

2. A figure of speech that uses *like* or *as* to compare two different things is a _____.
   A. limerick
   B. rhyme
   C. metaphor
   D. simile

3. *My heart is like a singing bird* is an example of a _____.
   A. signal
   B. simile
   C. melody
   D. lullaby

4. *A true friend is a bridge over troubled water* is a _____.
   A. simile
   B. fortune
   C. metaphor
   D. message

5. *The sun shone like a golden sword* is an example of a _____.
   A. sonnet
   B. metaphor
   C. simile
   D. memory

6. *The dog's ears fluttered like butterflies* is a _____.
   A. sign
   B. simile
   C. metaphor
   D. metropolis

GO ON

DIRECTIONS
Choose the correct word for each definition below. Circle the letter of the correct answer.

7. _____: show that something is important.
   A. exceed
   B. expand
   C. embroider
   D. emphasize

8. _____: the act of going to live in another country.
   A. donation
   B. destination
   C. cultivation
   D. immigration

9. _____: become larger.
   A. expand
   B. adjust
   C. salute
   D. lament

10. _____: make a change in something to make it better.
    A. adhere
    B. adjoin
    C. adopt
    D. adjust

11. _____: existing or happening for a short time only.
    A. history
    B. contrary
    C. mortuary
    D. temporary

DIRECTIONS
Choose the correctly spelled form of each word in bold type. Circle the letter of the correct answer.

12. **worry**
    A. worrys
    B. worries
    C. worris
    D. worriys

13. **family**
    A. families
    B. familys
    C. familees
    D. familyes

14. **funny**
    A. funner
    B. funnyer
    C. funneir
    D. funnier

15. **turkey**
    A. turkees
    B. turkies
    C. turkeys
    D. turkieys

16. **silly**
    A. silleest
    B. sillest
    C. silliest
    D. sillyest

READING: From *The Journal of Wong Ming-Chung*

DIRECTIONS
Choose the word or phrase that best answers each question. Circle the letter of the correct answer.

17. The story takes place in _____.
    A. China in the 18th century
    B. the gold mines in 1900
    C. San Francisco in 1852
    D. New York in the present time

18. Wong Ming-Chung feels trapped because he _____.
    A. has not passed his exams
    B. does not like living with his uncle
    C. does not have enough food to survive
    D. can't return home until he pays back what he owes

19. The narrator thinks he is standing in the middle of a forest because he is surrounded by _____.
    A. masts of ships
    B. huge crowds of people
    C. houses and apartments
    D. bugs

20. Which words best describe the weather in the story?
    A. hot and dry
    B. chilly
    C. snowy and icy cold
    D. sunny and warm

21. When they first arrive, the newcomers group together by _____.
    A. areas and family clans
    B. skills and interests
    C. age and physical strength
    D. level of education

22. Chinese stone masons built the first stone building because _____.
    A. there were no other stone masons
    B. the instructions were in Chinese
    C. the owner had fired everyone else
    D. the building was located in Chinatown

23. Wong Ming-Chung and his group stay _____.
    A. on the *Excalibur*
    B. in a small tent
    C. on Dupont Street
    D. inside the headquarters

GO ON

DIRECTIONS

Choose the adverb clause of time that best completes each sentence. Circle the letter of the correct answer.

24. Flowers start to bloom _____.
    A. in the neighbor's yard
    B. outside my window
    C. when spring arrives
    D. until the morning

25. Anita listens to the radio _____.
    A. on the table in her bedroom
    B. while she does her homework
    C. about the weather forecast
    D. and sings along with the songs

26. _____, she can see much better.
    A. Though the light is turned on
    B. Since she got glasses
    C. On a sunny beach
    D. Through the window

27. Toyo laughs loudly _____.
    A. and claps his hands
    B. after Rico tells a funny joke
    C. to swat at a fly on his head
    D. in his seat at the back of the room

28. _____, the sun comes out.
    A. Because she wished
    B. Through the curtains
    C. Over the mountain
    D. After a rainstorm

29. Let's take a walk _____.
    A. down the street
    B. before it gets dark
    C. and get some exercise
    D. in the park by the library

30. Eva listened _____.
    A. for the sound of footsteps
    B. on the bus to school
    C. while her friend talked
    D. through the open window

STOP

Unit 2 • Reading 4   Test   Grammar

UNIT 3

READING 1 TEST

KEY WORDS

DIRECTIONS
Choose the word that best completes each sentence. Circle the letter of the correct answer.

1. If you did something better than almost everyone else, it means that you _____.
   A. rebelled
   B. operated
   C. acquired
   D. excelled

2. A business or a project is called a(n) _____.
   A. satellite
   B. enterprise
   C. doctorate
   D. procedure

3. A picture that you make of yourself is a _____.
   A. still-life
   B. famine
   C. self-portrait
   D. self-esteem

4. Money awarded to pay for students' schooling is provided by _____.
   A. mosaics
   B. satellites
   C. scholarships
   D. monuments

5. A spacecraft that is sent into orbit around the earth or the moon is a _____.
   A. spangle
   B. famine
   C. satellite
   D. rocker

6. A time of hunger and lack of food is called a(n) _____.
   A. village
   B. famine
   C. enterprise
   D. program

GO ON

DIRECTIONS
Choose the correct word for each definition below. Circle the letter of the correct answer.

DIRECTIONS
Read each question below and find the correct answer. Circle the letter of the correct answer.

7. _____: money or help that is offered or given.
   A. restoration
   B. contribution
   C. constitution
   D. plantation

8. _____: the thing that you think is the most important.
   A. exhibit
   B. portrait
   C. priority
   D. sorority

9. _____: assistance, especially in the form of money, food, or equipment.
   A. aid
   B. wig
   C. alloy
   D. tools

10. _____: affecting or relating to the whole world.
    A. local
    B. feral
    C. global
    D. vocal

11. _____: a promise and a determination to do something.
    A. prototype
    B. contribution
    C. commitment
    B. advertisement

12. The prefix *re-* means "again." Which word means "to call again"?
    A. recall   C. intercall
    B. multicall   D. undercall

13. The prefix *inter-* means "between." Which word means "linked with others"?
    A. underlinked   C. relinked
    B. interlinked   D. multilinked

14. The prefix *multi-* means "many." Which word means "many levels"?
    A. relevel   C. underlevel
    B. interlevel   D. multilevel

15. The prefix *re-* means "again." Which word means "to find again"?
    A. underlocate   C. interlocate
    B. multilocate   D. relocate

16. The prefix *under-* means "below." Which word means "to go below"?
    A. repass   C. multipass
    B. underpass   D. interpass

17. The prefix *inter-* means "between." Which word means "a pause between periods of activity"?
    A. undermission   C. intermission
    B. remission   D. multimission

READING: "Success Stories"

DIRECTIONS
Choose the word or phrase that best completes each item or answers each question. Circle the letter of the correct answer.

18. When Frida Kahlo was in college, she _____.
    A. married Diego Rivera
    B. moved to a blue house
    C. got a disease called polio
    D. was in a terrible bus accident

19. Frida Kahlo is a famous _____.
    A. painter
    B. astronaut
    C. economist
    D. inventor

20. Bill Gates started the Microsoft Corporation in _____.
    A. 1955
    B. 1975
    C. 1985
    D. 2005

21. With the money that Muhammad Yunus lent them, the villagers _____.
    A. built wooden boats and caught fish
    B. made small stores and sold jewelry
    C. bought good land and planted wheat
    D. made bamboo stools and bought a cow

22. The Grameen Bank is not like other banks because it _____.
    A. gives very small loans
    B. gives animals, not money
    C. gives loans only to rich people
    D. does not need the loans paid back

23. After college, Mae Jamison _____.
    A. watched spaceflights on television
    B. moved to Decatur, Alabama, with her family
    C. moved to Chicago, Illinois, to attend school
    D. went to medical school and took engineering classes

GO ON

DIRECTIONS
Identify each underlined sentence part. Circle the letter of the correct answer.

24. <u>Mae Jemison is now a college professor</u>.
    A. subject pronoun
    B. relative pronoun
    C. dependent clause
    D. independent clause

25. Bill Gates started the Microsoft Corporation <u>that</u> developed Windows.
    A. independent clause
    B. dependent clause
    C. relative pronoun
    D. subject pronoun

26. Muhammad Yunus helped women <u>who were very poor</u>.
    A. independent clause
    B. dependent clause
    C. relative pronoun
    D. subject pronoun

27. <u>I want to see the tree</u> that was struck by lightning.
    A. independent clause
    B. dependent clause
    C. relative pronoun
    D. subject pronoun

28. The police are trying to find out <u>who stole the painting</u>.
    A. subject pronoun
    B. relative pronoun
    C. dependent clause
    D. independent clause

29. When the rink opens for the season, <u>we will go ice-skating</u>.
    A. subject pronoun
    B. relative pronoun
    C. dependent clause
    D. independent clause

30. You will be surprised when I tell you <u>who</u> I saw yesterday
    A. subject pronoun
    B. relative pronoun
    C. dependent clause
    D. independent clause

UNIT 3

READING 2 TEST

LITERARY WORDS

DIRECTIONS
Choose the word or words that best complete each sentence. Circle the letter of the correct answer.

1. Saying something again and again to emphasize an idea is called _____.
   A. duration
   B. repetition
   C. composition
   D. extension

2. A figure of speech in which one thing is spoken of as if it is something else for several lines or for an entire poem is called a(n) _____.
   A. extra offer
   B. exaggerated rhyme
   C. comparison
   D. extended metaphor

3. A group of lines in a poem is called a _____.
   A. lineage
   B. stanza
   C. sonnet
   D. tunic

4. *I eat my peas with honey;*
   I've done it all my life.
   It makes the peas taste funny,
   But it keeps them on the knife. is an example of _____.
   A. repetition
   B. a stanza
   C. a simile
   D. an extended metaphor

5. *Lost! All is lost! Even the kitchen sink—lost!* is an example of _____.
   A. repetition
   B. operation
   C. duration
   D. revision

6. *All the world's a stage*
   And all the men and women are
   merely players;
   They have their exits and entrances
   is an example of an _____.
   A. embossed line
   B. embroidered sentence
   C. comparison
   D. extended metaphor

GO ON

ACADEMIC WORDS

DIRECTIONS
Choose the correct word for each definition below. Circle the letter of the correct answer.

7. _____: clearly marking a person or thing as different from others.
   A. cultural
   B. instinctive
   C. maternal
   D. distinctive

8. _____: continue doing an activity or trying to achieve something.
   A. interpret
   B. pursue
   C. attend
   D. dismiss

9. _____: explain or translate.
   A. regret
   B. imagine
   C. interpret
   D. whittle

10. _____: related to a particular society and its way of life (arts, language, etc.).
   A. cultural
   B. mayoral
   C. federal
   D. agricultural

11. _____: exact and correct in every detail.
   A. similar
   B. distinctive
   C. precise
   D. prickly

WORD STUDY

DIRECTIONS
Choose the correct homophone for each word in bold type. Circle the letter of the correct answer.

12. **allowed**
   A. allot
   B. allied
   C. aloud
   D. allude

13. **eight**
   A. at
   B. eighth
   C. either
   D. ate

14. **break**
   A. broke
   B. brake
   C. brick
   D. brock

15. **herd**
   A. heard
   B. hearth
   C. hoard
   D. hard

16. **main**
   A. mine
   B. moon
   C. mainly
   D. mane

17. **soared**
   A. said
   B. sword
   C. soured
   D. soothe

READING: "An Interview with Naomi Shihab Nye" / "Making a Mosaic"

DIRECTIONS
Choose the word or phrase that best completes each item or answers each
question. Circle the letter of the correct answer.

"An Interview with Naomi Shihab Nye"

18. Naomi Shihab Nye attended high
     school in _____.
     A. Mexico
     B. St. Louis
     C. San Antonio
     D. Jerusalem

19. As a child, Naomi Shihab Nye wrote
     about _____.
     A. only pets
     B. Carl Sandburg
     C. typical kid stuff
     D. her Palestinian grandma

20. Naomi Shihab Nye was _____ when
     she published her first poem.
     A. seven years old
     B. fourteen years old
     C. twenty years old
     D. thirty years old

"Making a Mosaic"

21. In this poem, Naomi Shihab Nye
     describes broken plates and cups
     as _____.
     A. filthy
     B. lovely
     C. sharp
     D. shiny

22. Naomi Shihab Nye calls the two plates
     _____.
     A. "some people begin at the edge"
     B. "the story of my old days"
     C. "good things to play with"
     D. "a nice time, a terrible time"

23. The blue flowery plates are connected
     to _____.
     A. a relative's funeral
     B. a cancelled trip
     C. a ship that sunk
     D. a destroyed house

GO ON

DIRECTIONS
Choose the word or words that best complete each sentence. Circle the letter of the correct answer.

24. Luz avoided _____ the slippery parking lot.
    A. cross
    B. crossing
    C. crossed
    D. to cross

25. Making friends is easy, but _____ them takes work.
    A. keeps
    B. keep
    C. keeping
    D. kept

26. Jasper dislikes _____ late to class.
    A. arrive
    B. to arrive
    C. arrived
    D. arriving

27. The guitarist's _____ of that song was unique.
    A. playing
    B. play
    C. played
    D. plays

28. After the team lost, the coach said, "_____ isn't everything."
    A. Won
    B. Wins
    C. Winning
    D. Winned

29. Carla missed _____ a room with her sister.
    A. to share
    B. share
    C. shared
    D. sharing

30. _____ your dreams requires energy and determination.
    A. Following
    B. Follows
    C. Followed
    D. Follow

UNIT 3 — READING 3 TEST

LITERARY WORDS

DIRECTIONS
Choose the word or words that best complete each sentence. Circle the letter of the correct answer.

1. A feeling of excitement or curiosity about what is going to happen next in a piece of literature is called _____.
    A. simile
    B. suspense
    C. memento
    D. resolution

2. An explanation of why a character does certain things is called _____.
    A. caricature analysis
    B. character comparison
    C. character motivation
    D. character interest

3. *I heard a strange noise late at night, so I tiptoed to the door and twisted the handle* is an example of _____.
    A. suspense
    B. suffering
    C. climax
    D. resolution

4. *After seeing pictures of Chicago's skyscrapers, Dana can't wait to leave her small town* is an example of _____.
    A. character adventure
    B. character motivation
    C. character mobility
    D. character modernization

5. *Chris looks up slowly, wondering if he passed the big test* is an example of _____.
    A. suspense
    B. suspicion
    C. character flaws
    D. character motivation

6. *Jill likes to please people, so she always raises her hand, even when she doesn't know the answer* is an example of _____.
    A. character attitude
    B. character success
    C. character motivation
    D. suspense

GO ON

DIRECTIONS

Choose the correct word for each definition below. Circle the letter of the correct answer.

7. _____: be involved in a particular activity.
   A. relate
   B. insulate
   C. participate
   D. congratulate

8. _____: large enough to be noticed or have an effect.
   A. considerable
   B. affordable
   C. collapsible
   D. detachable

9. _____: goal; something that you are working hard to achieve.
   A. renegade
   B. contest
   C. objective
   D. champion

10. _____: happening before something else.
    A. accurate
    B. previous
    C. considerable
    D. devious

11. _____: put things where people could see them easily.
    A. weighed
    B. betrayed
    C. evaded
    D. displayed

DIRECTIONS

Choose the correctly spelled inflection for each of the bold type words below. Circle the letter of the correct answer.

12. **relay**
    A. relayd
    B. relayed
    C. relayyed
    D. relyed

13. **sip**
    A. sipped
    B. siped
    C. sipyed
    D. sipeed

14. **sob**
    A. sobing
    B. sobeing
    C. sobbying
    D. sobbing

15. **step**
    A. steppd
    B. steped
    C. stepped
    D. steping

16. **bump**
    A. bummped
    B. bumpd
    C. bumped
    D. bummed

17. **tag**
    A. taged
    B. tagied
    C. tagged
    D. taggied

READING: "The Marble Champp"

DIRECTIONS

Choose the phrase that best completes each item or answers each question. Circle the letter of the correct answer.

18. The mayor had given Lupe a small trophy for _____.
    A. excellent school attendance
    B. raising wasps for the science fair
    C. being an outstanding softball player
    D. winning a soccer championship

19. Lupe makes her wrists stronger by _____.
    A. washing the dishes for a week
    B. eating dinner with her left hand
    C. doing push-ups with her fingertips
    D. playing marbles with her brother

20. Lupe's father helps her reach her goal by _____.
    A. giving her an eraser to squeeze
    B. taking her to play racquetball
    C. taking her to the doctor
    D. putting light in the backyard so she can practice after dark

21. Lupe felt sorry for the first girl she played against because the girl _____.
    A. never smiled
    B. had a broken thumb
    C. had no one to cheer for her
    D. did not have enough marbles

22. Lupe's final opponent is _____.
    A. her neighbor Alfonso
    B. Miss Baseball Cap
    C. the winner of the boy's division
    D. the President of the Marble Association

23. Lupe won the marbles championship because she _____.
    A. read a book about marbles
    B. watched her brother
    C. played sports
    D. practiced a lot

GO ON

GRAMMAR

DIRECTIONS

Choose the phrase that best completes each sentence. Circle the letter of the correct answer.

24. _____ is the best part of Marisa's day.
    A. To follow all around
    B. To capture a few
    C. To watch the sunrise
    D. To do the same thing

25. Cleo can afford _____ for the tickets.
    A. to see
    B. to pay
    C. to remind
    D. to fold

26. I listen to music _____.
    A. to relax
    B. to greet
    C. to speak
    D. to win

27. Min Jung managed _____ the assignment on time.
    A. to disregard
    B. to forget
    C. to crash
    D. to complete

28. _____ other people is very worthwhile.
    A. To give
    B. To help
    C. To talk
    D. To move

29. Sergey went outside _____.
    A. to watch television
    B. to rake the yard
    C. to turn and go
    D. to come back in

30. I offered _____ because her car was being repaired.
    A. to read
    B. to decide
    C. to drive
    D. to fix

Name _____ Date _____

UNIT **3** **READING 4 TEST**

KEY WORDS

DIRECTIONS
Choose the word that best completes each sentence. Circle the letter
of the correct answer.

1. The science of creating a human-like
   machine is called _____.
   A. athletics
   B. robotics
   C. physics
   D. theories

2. Someone who designs, builds, and
   repairs bridges and machines is called
   a(n) _____.
   A. engineer
   B. physicist
   C. carpenter
   D. doctor

3. Ideas about how something works or
   why something happens are _____.
   A. melodies
   B. fantasies
   C. theories
   D. robotics

4. The creation of a new idea, method, or
   invention is called a(n) _____.
   A. corporation
   B. innovation
   C. transformer
   D. arrangement

5. Someone who studies the way the
   physical world works, involving things
   such as light, energy, and movement, is
   a(n) _____.
   A. engineer
   B. astronaut
   C. physicist
   D. psychologist

6. A large company or group of
   companies that is allowed to act as a
   single business is a _____.
   A. corporation
   B. cosmetic
   C. coliseum
   D. community

GO ON

Copyright © by Pearson Education, Inc.

Unit 3 • Reading 4 Test Key Words **79**

DIRECTIONS

Choose the correct word for each definition. Circle the letter of the correct answer.

7. _____: a difficult task or problem.
   A. theory
   B. design
   C. challenge
   D. decision

8. _____: succeed in getting something you want.
   A. retain
   B. affect
   C. create
   D. attain

9. _____: a plan or sketch.
   A. design
   B. puzzle
   C. decoy
   D. signature

10. _____: influence; produce a change.
    A. affect
    B. intend
    C. attain
    D. agree

11. _____: knowledge or understanding.
    A. fairness
    B. vastness
    C. awareness
    D. greatness

DIRECTIONS

Choose the language of origin for each of the bold type words. Circle the letter of the correct answer.

12. **tycoon**
    A. Japanese
    B. French
    C. Spanish
    D. African

13. **safari**
    A. French
    B. Chinese
    C. Swahili
    D. Italian

14. **cafeteria**
    A. Chinese
    B. Russian
    C. Arabic
    D. Spanish

15. **zero**
    A. French
    B. Arabic
    C. Spanish
    D. Russian

16. **volcano**
    A. German
    B. Chinese
    C. Italian
    D. Spanish

17. **tea**
    A. Spanish
    B. Chinese
    C. French
    D. Arabic

Name _____ Date _____

DIRECTIONS
Choose the phrase that best completes each item or answers each question. Circle the letter of the correct answer.

18. The team's 2004 win was a "stunning upset" because the students _____.
    A. worked on their own without any adults
    B. entered the competition at the very last minute
    C. had never before competed in a national contest
    D. beat out high schools and universities from across the U.S.

19. For this year's challenge, the robot needs to be able to _____.
    A. read a book to a vision-impaired person
    B. prepare a meal and then wash all the dishes
    C. fill small bottles with an exact amount of a clear liquid
    D. shoot soft foam balls through a hole in a clear plastic wall

20. What famous school does the Carl Hayden robotics team regularly compete with?
    A. MIT
    B. Harvard
    C. Cal Tech
    D. NY Tech

21. The team's robot, "Karen," is named after _____.
    A. a teammate who died
    B. the team's mentor
    C. the school's principal
    D. the person who bought the team's T-shirts

22. How are robots used today?
    A. They are used in all action movies instead of actors.
    B. They are used as sophisticated human-like creatures.
    C. They are used in factories to do routine or dangerous jobs.
    D. They are used to take care of sick people in hospitals.

23. How do engineers make our lives better?
    A. Engineers create practical solutions to real-world problems.
    B. Engineers raise flowers and plants that make the world beautiful.
    C. Engineers interpret the laws and help people understand the rules.
    D. Engineers invent new medicines to help sick people get better.

GO ON

DIRECTIONS
Choose the word or words that best complete each sentence. Circle the letter of the correct answer.

24. _____ student can succeed.
    A. All
    B. Every
    C. Most
    D. One of

25. Anita likes _____ classes.
    A. every
    B. one of
    C. none
    D. both

26. _____ Germany and France use the Euro.
    A. All
    B. Both
    C. One of
    D. Every

27. _____ of the clouds look fluffy.
    A. All
    B. Every
    C. Various
    D. A little

28. Saji has _____ friends.
    A. most
    B. one of
    C. every
    D. several

29. _____ days are sunny in summer.
    A. Every
    B. One of
    C. Most
    D. Both

30. _____ assignment is important.
    A. Most
    B. Every
    C. All
    D. Both

STOP

Name _____ Date _____

UNIT 4

READING 1 TEST

KEY WORDS

DIRECTIONS
Choose the word or words that best complete each sentence. Circle the letter of the correct answer.

1. Using the sun to produce energy is called _____.
   A. sonar detection
   B. fossil fuels
   C. solar power
   D. heat waves

2. Something made from a mixture of two or more things is called a _____.
   A. chasm
   B. hybrid
   C. vehicle
   D. fertilizer

3. Something so small that it can only be seen with special instruments is called _____.
   A. epic
   B. philanthropic
   C. microscopic
   D. photographic

4. Things found in a country that can be used to increase its wealth, such as oil, coal, or useful land, are called _____.
   A. resources
   B. receptions
   C. standards
   D. treaties

5. Something put on soil to make plants grow is called _____.
   A. hybrid
   B. vaporizer
   C. fertilizer
   D. moisturizer

6. Fuel that was formed from the remains of plants and animals from long ago is called _____.
   A. black gold
   B. solar power
   C. fertilizer
   D. fossil fuels

GO ON

DIRECTIONS

Choose the correct word or words for each definition. Circle the letter of the correct answer.

7. _____: concentrate on or give special attention to.
   A. focus on
   B. enable
   C. decide on
   D. extract

8. _____: ways of relating, such as speaking or writing.
   A. regulation
   B. formation
   C. substitution
   D. communication

9. _____: make something possible.
   A. elevate
   B. allow
   C. improve
   D. enable

10. _____: something you can use or do instead of something else.
    A. alternative
    B. deception
    C. additive
    D. regulation

11. _____: official rule or order.
    A. concentration
    B. regulation
    C. decoration
    D. federation

DIRECTIONS

Read each question and find the correct answer. Circle the letter of the correct answer.

12. Which is the noun form of *pollute*?
    A. pollutative
    B. polluted
    C. pollution
    D. pollutatory

13. Which is the noun form of *transport*?
    A. transportational
    B. transported
    C. transportedly
    D. transportation

14. Which is the noun form of *combine*?
    A. combined
    B. combination
    C. combinable
    D. combining

15. Which is the adjective form of *pollute*?
    A. polluted
    B. pollution
    C. polute
    D. pollutingly

16. Which is the adjective form of *produce*?
    A. productative
    B. produced
    C. production
    D. producing

GO ON

READING: "Changing Earth"

DIRECTIONS
Choose the word or phrase that best completes each item or answers each question. Circle the letter of the correct answer.

17. How has Earth's population changed in the last 200 years?
    A. It has shrunk from 4 million people to 1 million people.
    B. It has shrunk from 4 billion people to 1 billion people.
    C. It has grown from 1 million people to 6 million people.
    D. It has grown from 1 billion people to 6 billion people.

18. Water and air became polluted because of a lack of knowledge and _____.
    A. bigger buildings
    B. limited technologies
    C. reduced fossil fuels
    D. extreme weather

19. Scientists are changing the food supply through _____.
    A. fossil fuels
    B. solar energy
    C. genetic engineering
    D. general technology

20. What do some people think of these changes to the food supply?
    A. They think these changes will not have an effect on other living things.
    B. They think these changes will not harm the environment in any way.
    C. They think it is a mistake to change the characteristics of a plant or animal.
    D. They think these changes will help stop pollution in inexpensive ways.

21. What happens to the chemicals on plants when water washes them away?
    A. They dissolve into the soil.
    B. They pollute rivers and lakes.
    C. They evaporate into the atmosphere.
    D. They cover all the fruits and vegetables.

22. Scientists are experimenting with solar and hydrogen energy to power _____.
    A. cars
    B. bicycles
    C. computers
    D. crops

23. Solar and wind power are good because they _____.
    A. are clean
    B. consume energy
    C. are always available
    D. do not depend on natural forces

GO ON

DIRECTIONS

Choose the correct words or phrase that best completes each sentence. Circle the letter of the correct answer.

24. The school _____ Raoul a scholarship yet.
    A. haven't gived
    B. hasn't gave
    C. haven't given
    D. hasn't given

25. The doctor _____ over 1,000 patients.
    A. has treat
    B. have treated
    C. has treated
    D. is treated

26. The students _____ on two field trips so far this year.
    A. have went
    B. have gone
    C. has went
    D. has gone

27. _____ Lisa yet?
    A. Have you called
    B. Has you call
    C. Have you call
    D. Has you called

28. They _____ the winter in Florida for the past ten years.
    A. has spend
    B. have spend
    C. have spent
    D. has spent

29. Chandra _____ that song since she was a little girl.
    A. has sang
    B. have sing
    C. have sung
    D. has sung

30. I _____ my English a lot this year.
    A. have improves
    B. is improved
    C. have improved
    D. has improved

STOP

UNIT 4 — READING 2 TEST

LITERARY WORDS

DIRECTIONS
Choose the word that best completes each sentence. Circle the letter of the correct answer.

1. A struggle between opposing forces is called _____.
   A. resolution
   B. strategy
   C. conflict
   D. foreshadowing

2. A hint or clue in a story about what will happen later on is called _____.
   A. backing
   B. underpinning
   C. shadowboxing
   D. foreshadowing

3. *Marcella shouted at her brother, "Why do you always forget to put the milk back in the refrigerator?"* is an example of _____.
   A. conflict
   B. judgment
   C. conspiracy
   D. combustion

4. *People in the town usually smiled and waved, but today everyone stayed behind locked doors* is an example of _____.
   A. conflict
   B. stereotyping
   C. celebrating
   D. foreshadowing

5. *Nikos believed it would be a wonderful day. He was too happy to notice the dark clouds on the horizon* is an example of _____.
   A. conflict
   B. skepticism
   C. foreshadowing
   D. procrastination

6. *After arguing over the telephone, Marta decided not to attend her sister's party* is an example of _____.
   A. conflict
   B. foreshadowing
   C. wiretapping
   D. consideration

GO ON

DIRECTIONS

Choose the correct word for each definition below. Circle the letter of the correct answer.

7. _____: something that happens, especially something that is unusual.
   A. incident
   B. impact
   C. outcome
   D. consequence

8. _____: harmed or wounded in an accident.
   A. tainted
   B. injured
   C. intercepted
   D. disturbed

9. _____: something that happens as a result of a particular action.
   A. impact
   B. annoyance
   C. happenstance
   D. consequence

10. _____: final result.
    A. impact
    B. collision
    C. outcome
    D. response

11. _____: effect that an event or situation has on someone or something.
    A. impact
    B. contract
    C. sensation
    D. consequence

12. _____: succeed in doing or gaining something.
    A. deceive
    B. achieve
    C. perceive
    D. acknowledge

DIRECTIONS

Choose the correct synonym of the word in bold type. Circle the letter of the correct answer.

13. **difficult**
    A. hard
    B. short
    C. easy
    D. real

14. **stare**
    A. blink
    B. gaze
    C. glance
    D. wink

15. **jump**
    A. bend
    B. nod
    C. swing
    D. leap

16. **home**
    A. half
    B. happy
    C. house
    D. hallway

Name _____ Date _____

DIRECTIONS
Choose the phrase that best completes each item or answers each question. Circle the letter of the correct answer.

17. In the first letter, what does Jason Winthrop ask people to do?
    A. He asks them to buy a car.
    B. He asks them to slow down.
    C. He asks them to use another street.
    D. He asks them to wash their horses.

18. When was the first letter written?
    A. It was written in 1800.
    B. It was written in 1900.
    C. It was written in 1950.
    D. It was written in 2000.

19. Jason Winthrop, Jr. thinks the reason for traffic problems is that there are _____.
    A. not enough traffic lights
    B. poorly built bumpy roads
    C. too many horses that stop traffic
    D. more and more people moving to the area

20. What does Jason Winthrop, Jr. say about pollution?
    A. He says that large factories are causing a great deal of air pollution.
    B. He says that it is not a major factor, and likely won't be in the future.
    C. He asks people to take buses and trolleys to reduce air pollution.
    D. He asks people to stop blowing their horns and causing noise pollution.

21. Jason Winthrop III does not want to sell his house because _____.
    A. it has always brought him good luck
    B. it is not worth the money he wants for it
    C. it has belonged to his family for a long time
    D. it is admired by people who work in the city

22. According to the third letter, what did people think would cut the number of accidents in half?
    A. They thought using airplanes would cut the number of accidents in half.
    B. They thought waving their arms would cut the number of accidents in half.
    C. They thought a flashing light would cut the number of accidents in half.
    D. They thought a one-way street would cut the number of accidents in half.

23. After reading the three letters, we understand that _____.
    A. horses are better transportation than cars
    B. people caused the traffic problems at the intersection
    C. the Winthrops exaggerated the problem at the intersection
    D. technology solved the traffic problems at the intersection

DIRECTIONS

Choose the words or phrase that best completes each sentence. Circle the letter of the correct answer.

24. Scientists are sure that the world's population _____ next year.
    A. will increase
    B. won't increase
    C. probably will increase
    D. probably won't increase

25. Biologists suspect that mountain gorillas _____ in the next five years if laws are not passed to help them.
    A. won't become extinct
    B. will become extinct
    C. will probably become extinct
    D. probably won't become extinct

26. I am really not sure if the traffic light will make people drive more carefully; _____.
    A. it will.
    B. maybe it won't
    C. probably it will
    D. probably it won't

27. Felicia isn't sure, but she _____ to the party because she has a lot of homework.
    A. will go
    B. won't go
    C. probably won't go
    D. probably will go

28. I am certain that I _____ the concert because I don't enjoy that kind of music.
    A. will attend
    B. won't attend
    C. probably will attend
    D. probably won't attend

29. Natasha looks a little tired. She _____ quickly tonight.
    A. will fall asleep
    B. won't fall asleep
    C. probably won't fall asleep
    D. will probably fall asleep

30. I'm busy right now, so I _____ you tomorrow; I promise.
    A. will call
    B. won't call
    C. will probably call
    D. probably won't call

UNIT 4 — READING 3 TEST

KEY WORDS

DIRECTIONS
Choose the word or words that best complete each sentence. Circle the letter of the correct answer.

1. Groups of soldiers are called _____.
   A. pods
   B. herds
   C. troops
   D. justices

2. Unfair treatment of people based on their race is called _____.
   A. recidivism
   B. racism
   C. radiation
   D. segregation

3. The court that decides questions of federal law is called _____.
   A. federal court
   B. judicial palace
   C. state house
   D. federal square

4. Rights guaranteed by the U.S. Constitution are called _____.
   A. labor laws
   B. national rights
   C. social laws
   D. civil rights

5. Judges in a court of law are called _____.
   A. justices
   B. attorneys
   C. lawyers
   D. geniuses

6. The practice of forcing people of different racial groups to live apart from each other or to go to separate schools is called _____.
   A. motivation
   B. integration
   C. segregation
   D. compensation

GO ON

ACADEMIC WORDS

DIRECTIONS
Choose the correct word for each definition below. Circle the letter of the correct answer.

7. _____: make someone believe.
   A. convince
   B. contrast
   C. confirm
   D. conclude

8. _____: start to do something.
   A. celebrate
   B. incubate
   C. undertake
   D. integrate

9. _____: very large in size or amount.
   A. apparent
   B. enormous
   C. important
   D. unanimous

10. _____: easy to understand; obvious.
    A. opaque
    B. brilliant
    C. enormous
    D. apparent

11. _____: a picture, a letter, or a sign that means or stands for something else.
    A. seal
    B. tariff
    C. leaflet
    D. symbol

12. _____: unite; end the practice of separating people of different races.
    A. integrate
    B. segregate
    C. celebrate
    D. appreciate

WORD STUDY

DIRECTIONS
Read the words in each item below. Circle the letter of the words that should be capitalized.

13. A. cemetery
    B. canadian
    C. village
    D. computer

14. A. their teacher
    B. my father
    C. her little sister
    D. dr. michael carvo

15. A. the big wall
    B. a famous statue
    C. a huge monument
    D. empire state building

16. A. beach
    B. friendship
    C. vietnam war
    D. big marathon

Name _____ Date _____

DIRECTIONS

Choose the word or phrase that best completes each item or answers each question. Circle the letter of the correct answer.

17. In _____ the Supreme Court said that black and white students had to be educated together.
    A. 1945
    B. 1954
    C. 1965
    D. 1975

18. What were the nine black students enrolled in a white high school called?
    A. They were called the "Brave Nine."
    B. They were called the "Proud Ones."
    C. They were called the "Little Rock Nine."
    D. They were called the "Courageous Ones."

19. What did black children have to do to be admitted to white schools in New Orleans?
    A. They had to pass a test.
    B. They had to give a speech.
    C. They had to get dressed up.
    D. They had to move to a new home.

20. Rudy Bridges attended kindergarten at _____.
    A. William Frantz Public School
    B. the Louisiana Free School
    C. Little Rock Elementary School
    D. Johnson Lockett Elementary School

21. Who wanted Ruby to attend the school with the white students?
    A. Ruby's brother wanted her to attend the school with the white students.
    B. Ruby's mother wanted her to attend the school with the white students.
    C. Ruby's father wanted her to attend the school with the white students.
    D. Ruby's teacher wanted her to attend the school with the white students.

22. On her first day of school at William Frantz, Ruby drove to school with her mother and _____.
    A. NAACP leaders
    B. her teacher
    C. two classmates
    D. federal marshals

23. What did Ruby think people were doing when she arrived at William Frantz?
    A. She thought they were fighting.
    B. She thought they were playing.
    C. She thought they were celebrating.
    D. She thought they were studying.

GRAMMAR

DIRECTIONS

Choose the word that best completes each sentence. Circle the letter of the correct answer.

24. Sylvie learned to ski, write poetry, cook a meal, _____ play the flute this year.
    - A. but
    - B. and
    - C. or
    - D. none of the above

25. I will ask either my brother _____ my sister to drive me to school.
    - A. but
    - B. and
    - C. or
    - D. none of the above

26. Let's eat _____ this delicious dinner.
    - A. and
    - B. or
    - C. but
    - D. none of the above

27. Please listen to her speech _____ write down what she says.
    - A. and
    - B. but
    - C. or
    - D. none of the above

28. Rita can either go to sleep early, _____ she can stay up late.
    - A. and
    - B. but
    - C. or
    - D. none of the above

29. Would you like to play at the park _____ then visit the museum?
    - A. and
    - B. but
    - C. or
    - D. none of the above

30. She could have won _____ if she had prepared.
    - A. and
    - B. but
    - C. or
    - D. none of the above

STOP

READING 4 TEST

LITERARY WORDS

DIRECTIONS
Choose the word that best completes each sentence. Circle the letter of the correct answer.

1. The repetition of sounds is called
    _____.
    A. theme
    B. rhythm
    C. topic
    D. rhyme

2. The central idea, or message, of a work
    of literature is called the _____.
    A. plot
    B. theme
    C. rhyme
    D. symbol

3. *Hark! Hark! The dogs do bark* is an
    example of a _____.
    A. theme
    B. proverb
    C. rhyme
    D. lyric

4. *Helping friends who are in trouble* is an
    example of a _____.
    A. fact
    B. rhyme
    C. thicket
    D. theme

5. *Grab your yellow mat and your floppy
    hat. Let's go to the beach; it's not far to
    reach* is an example of a _____.
    A. simile
    B. rhyme
    C. theme
    D. thistle

6. *If you work hard, your dreams will come
    true* is an example of a _____.
    A. rhyme
    B. theme
    C. legend
    D. limerick

ACADEMIC WORDS

DIRECTIONS
Choose the correct word for each definition below. Circle the letter of the correct answer.

7. _____: all the people who live in the same area or town.
   A. cathedral
   B. commotion
   C. community
   D. tenement

8. _____: printed and sold a book, newspaper, or magazine.
   A. published
   B. polished
   C. presented
   D. demolished

9. _____: lasting a short time.
   A. rigid
   B. brief
   C. stately
   D. extended

10. _____: one part of something.
    A. constable
    B. section
    C. ligament
    D. ditch

11. _____: referring to a place that is made up of homes, not offices or businesses.
    A. urban
    B. holistic
    C. reserved
    D. residential

WORD STUDY

DIRECTIONS
Find the word with a long *e* sound. Circle the letter of the correct answer.

12. A. melt
    B. deal
    C. fed
    D. depth

13. A. peel
    B. desk
    C. kept
    D. red

14. A. taffy
    B. rhyme
    C. except
    D. better

15. A. whey
    B. why
    C. we
    D. when

16. A. pencil
    B. type
    C. temper
    D. clean

READING 4: "Harlem: Then and Now"/*Tar Beach*/"Harlem" and "Dreams"

DIRECTIONS

Choose the word or phrase that best completes each item or answers each question. Circle the letter of the correct answer.

"Harlem: Then and Now"

17. When he wrote this essay, how old was James Baldwin?
    A. He was 13 years old.
    B. He was 20 years old.
    C. He was 30 years old.
    D. He was 40 years old.

18. What was Harlem like in the early 1600s?
    A. It was rich farmland.
    B. It was a wilderness.
    C. It was a bustling city.
    D. It was a Dutch colony.

19. By the nineteenth century, what had disappeared from Harlem?
    A. Hills had disappeared.
    B. Stores had disappeared.
    C. Mansions had disappeared.
    D. Muddy roads had disappeared.

20. What does Baldwin hope will be a part of Harlem's future?
    A. He hopes farming will be a part of Harlem's future.
    B. He hopes growth and improvement will be a part of Harlem's future.
    C. He hopes better streets and playgrounds will be a part of Harlem's future.
    D. He hopes a return to the lifestyle of the past will be part of Harlem's future.

"Tar Beach"

21. In this poem, flying is a symbol for _____.
    A. fear
    B. magic
    C. freedom
    D. technology

"Harlem"

22. In this poem, Hughes infers that it is important _____.
    A. not to give up dreams
    B. to dream of raisins and sweets
    C. to keep all your food refrigerated
    D. to not put off achieving your dreams

"Dreams"

23. In this poem, what is a life without dreams compared to?
    A. It is compared to a barren field.
    B. It is compared to a singing bird.
    C. It is compared to a syrupy sweet.
    D. It is compared to a life with dreams.

GO ON

GRAMMAR

DIRECTIONS
Choose the word that best completes each sentence. Circle the letter of the correct answer.

24. Hakim is very lucky because _____ best friend lives next door.
    A. their
    B. our
    C. his
    D. its

25. We just moved here. _____ new neighbor is from Egypt.
    A. Our
    B. Their
    C. Ours
    D. My

26. I like ice cream. _____ favorite flavor is strawberry.
    A. Your
    B. Our
    C. Her
    D. My

27. Thank you for letting me use _____ pencil.
    A. yours
    B. your
    C. their
    D. he

28. They have a piano in _____ living room.
    A. my
    B. his
    C. their
    D. our

29. She likes to ride _____ bike around the block.
    A. her
    B. their
    C. hers
    D. its

30. That bird is beautiful because _____ feathers are very colorful.
    A. it
    B. its
    C. your
    D. our

Name _____ Date _____

LITERARY WORDS

DIRECTIONS
Choose the word or words that best complete each sentence. Circle the letter of the correct answer.

1. A conversation between characters is called a _____.
   A. monologue
   B. prologue
   C. flashback
   D. dialogue

2. A scene from the past that interrupts the sequence of events is called a

   _____.
   A. flashlight
   B. flashback
   C. dialogue
   D. symbol

3. *"Would you like to join our club?"* Nadia asked. *"Of course I would!"* exclaimed *Betsy*, is an example of _____.
   A. a flashback
   B. a flare-up
   C. dialogue
   D. elegance

4. *The boys laughing and playing baseball made the old man remember his first baseball game on that warm, sunny day, long ago,* is an example of _____.
   A. flashback
   B. flash flood
   C. whiplash
   D. backlash

5. *"Let's go sled riding,"* Vikram said. *"Sounds great to me!"* Anil answered is an example of _____.
   A. catalog
   B. dialogue
   C. agony
   D. analog

6. *As Sarah drifted to sleep, she returned to those days at her grandma's house in the countryside* is an example of _____.
   A. dialogue
   B. childhood
   C. flashback
   D. flashforward

GO ON

ACADEMIC WORDS

DIRECTIONS
Choose the correct word for each definition below. Circle the letter of the correct answer.

7. _____: help.
   A. locate
   B. profit
   C. assist
   D. accompany

8. _____: someone who translates the spoken words in one language into another language.
   A. interpreter
   B. contributor
   C. distributor
   D. broadcaster

9. _____: go somewhere with someone.
   A. accompany
   B. accentuate
   C. flabbergast
   D. guarantee

10. _____: find the exact position.
    A. assist
    B. lodge
    C. locate
    D. accelerate

11. _____: something you want to do in the future.
    A. gourd
    B. goal
    C. colt
    D. mole

WORD STUDY

DIRECTIONS
Choose the synonym for each word in bold type. Circle the letter of the correct answer.

12. **enemy**
    A. foe
    B. crowd
    C. people
    D. friend

13. **yell**
    A. mumble
    B. shout
    C. whisper
    D. speak

14. **interpret**
    A. plead
    B. break
    C. throw
    D. translate

15. **leave**
    A. depart
    B. delete
    C. return
    D. attend

16. **explore**
    A. travel
    B. toddle
    C. advance
    D. experiment

READING: From *River to Tomorrow*/"River Song"/
"Morning Prayer Song"

DIRECTIONS
Choose the word or phrase that best completes each item or answers each question. Circle the letter of the correct answer.

"River to Tomorrow"

17. How long ago was Sacagawea kidnapped?
    A. She was kidnapped 1 year ago.
    B. She was kidnapped 5 years ago.
    C. She was kidnapped 10 years ago.
    D. She was kidnapped 10 years ago.

18. Sacagawea is important to Lewis and Clark because _____.
    A. she can find food no one else can find and cook it well
    B. she can make moccasins to protect the explorers' feet
    C. she can paint beautiful pictures of what the explorers see
    D. she can improve chances that the Shoshone will trade with the explorers

19. The Shoshone sign of peace is _____.
    A. planting three small, thin pine trees
    B. drawing maps in the dusty brown earth
    C. clapping your hands twice and facing east
    D. holding a blanket a specific way three times

20. How did Sacagawea know that her people had visited the place by the river?
    A. They had carved symbols in large, flat rocks.
    B. They had stripped the bark from pine trees.
    C. They had left a canoe at the river's edge.
    D. They had left a pair of Shoshone moccasins.

21. The Shoshone chief who spoke to Captain Clark's men was Sacagawea's _____.
    A. father
    B. husband
    C. uncle
    D. brother

"River Song"

22. In this poem, memories are compared to _____.
    A. love's melodies
    B. an old rolling river
    C. light in a fading sky
    D. dancing springtime waters

"Morning Prayer Song"

23. Who are the people praying to in this poem?
    A. They are praying to Mother Earth.
    B. They are praying to their children.
    C. They are praying to each other.
    D. They are praying to the songs they love.

GO ON

DIRECTIONS

Choose the word or words that best complete each sentence. Circle the letter of the correct answer.

24. _____ she arrived, everyone had left.
    A. During
    B. By the time
    C. At first
    D. At night

25. _____ the movie ended, many people had fallen asleep.
    A. At first
    B. Before
    C. Because
    D. Due to

26. Before Marisa _____ at home, the dog _____ her sock.
    A. arrived/ate
    B. had arrived/eaten
    C. had arrived/had eaten
    D. arrived/had eaten

27. At first, learning English _____ difficult, but then it _____ easier.
    A. been/had become
    B. had been/became
    C. had been/had become
    D. been/became

28. Lenny _____ about what to write before he _____ his essay.
    A. thought/had started
    B. had thought/had started
    C. had thought/started
    D. thought/started

29. Mrs. Kim _____ working by the time her daughter _____ home.
    A. finished/had come
    B. had finished/had come
    C. had finished/came
    D. finished/came

30. Before they _____ on vacation, they _____ what to take with them.
    A. had gone/decided
    B. had gone/had decided
    C. went/had decided
    D. went/decided

Name _____ Date _____

READING 2 TEST

KEY WORDS

DIRECTIONS
Choose the word or words that best complete each sentence. Circle the letter of the correct answer.

1. A unit for measuring length equal to 1,000 meters is called a _____.
    A. scale
    B. longitude
    C. metabolism
    D. kilometer

2. To measure the distances on a map you would use a _____.
    A. relief
    B. vanity
    C. scale
    D. colic

3. The average level of the sea is called _____.
    A. sea level
    B. seaward
    C. seamstress
    D. sea urchin

4. The differences in height or depth of hills, valleys, and other features in an area is shown on a _____ map.
    A. plain
    B. relieve
    C. cleft
    D. relief

5. Something relating to geography is _____.
    A. genetic
    B. economical
    C. geographical
    D. generational

6. The measurement of height above sea level is called _____.
    A. equation
    B. territory
    C. elevation
    D. kilometer

GO ON

DIRECTIONS

Choose the correct word for each definition below. Circle the letter of the correct answer.

7. _____: destroy gradually by wind, rain, or acid.
   A. detach
   B. elude
   C. erode
   D. stifle

8. _____: relating to the body, not the mind.
   A. audible
   B. physical
   C. chemical
   D. historical

9. _____: information that is shown in the form of pictures, graphs, etc.
   A. outline
   B. plug
   C. frame
   D. chart

10. _____: very close or next to.
    A. between
    B. remote
    C. affluent
    D. adjacent

11. _____: written words or phrases that name or describe something.
    A. labels
    B. cables
    C. fables
    D. columns

12. _____: discovered by searching or by chance.
    A. misplaced
    B. found
    C. eroded
    D. framed

DIRECTIONS

Read each question below and find the correct answer. Circle the letter of the correct answer.

13. Which word has a long *a* sound?
    A. bias
    B. relieve
    C. ladder
    D. weight

14. Which word has a long *a* sound?
    A. feint
    B. tier
    C. feat
    D. drier

15. Which word has a long *e* sound?
    A. pelt
    B. pear
    C. pier
    D. pyre

16. Which word has a long *e* sound?
    A. negligible
    B. freight
    C. neighbor
    D. bandolier

GO ON

Name _____ Date _____

DIRECTIONS
Choose the word or phrase that best completes each item or answers each question. Circle the letter of the correct answer.

17. What does the key on a relief map show?
    A. It shows the direction that you are facing.
    B. It shows how high the land is above sea level.
    C. It shows how many miles equal a certain distance.
    D. It shows the difference between features and regions.

18. A scale on a map shows _____.
    A. distance
    B. elevation
    C. climate
    D. geology

19. Elevation can be measured in _____.
    A. yards or miles
    B. leaps or bounds
    C. ounces or liters
    D. feet or meters

20. Most land in the United States is _____.
    A. at sea level
    B. below sea level
    C. above sea level
    D. close to sea level

21. Where does a compass point?
    A. It points to the Atlantic Ocean.
    B. It points to your home.
    C. It points to the planet Saturn.
    D. It points to the North Pole.

22. What allowed explorers to take an accurate reading from their compasses?
    A. A magnet and a lodestone allowed them to take an accurate reading.
    B. A stone glued below the case allowed them to take an accurate reading.
    C. A round card fixed to the needle allowed them to take an accurate reading.
    D. A needle attached to a rubber band allowed them to take an accurate reading.

23. When you make a compass, how do you magnetize the needle?
    A. You move the magnet over its tip.
    B. You push the needle into the cork.
    C. You put the needle into water.
    D. You place the water on the desk.

GO ON

GRAMMAR

DIRECTIONS
Choose the word or words that best complete each sentence. Circle the letter of the correct answer.

24. _____ directions to the festival.
   A. Please get
   B. Please see
   C. Please say
   D. Please think

25. _____ the book on the desk.
   A. Sit
   B. Pick
   C. Put
   D. Look

26. _____ the answer by tomorrow.
   A. Think
   B. Find
   C. Ask
   D. Please

27. _____ the food before it gets cold.
   A. Please
   B. See
   C. Cook
   D. Eat

28. _____ me the homework.
   A. Please tell
   B. Please explain
   C. Please talk
   D. Please speak

29. Gently _____ the wheel.
   A. circle
   B. survey
   C. turn
   D. ignore

30. Please _____ me how to bake a cake.
   A. draw
   B. show
   C. point
   D. let

UNIT 5

READING 3 TEST

KEY WORDS

DIRECTIONS
Choose the word that best completes each sentence. Circle the letter of the correct answer.

1. When you gather crops from the field, you have _____ them.
   A. harvested
   B. sheltered
   C. insulated
   D. swindled

2. People who go to live in a new country, colony, or region are called _____.
   A. settlers
   B. brokers
   C. commanders
   D. stockholders

3. Freedom from being controlled by other people or governments is called _____.
   A. fragmentation
   B. attendance
   C. justification
   D. independence

4. Farmers who rent land to farm and pay the owners with a portion of the crops they grow are called _____.
   A. missionaries
   B. sharecroppers
   C. interpreters
   D. plowshares

5. People sent out by a church to spread its religion in a foreign country are called _____.
   A. diplomats
   B. celebrities
   C. missionaries
   D. sharecroppers

6. Working on a large farm where cattle, horses, or sheep are raised is called _____.
   A. reforming
   B. wandering
   C. ranching
   D. trampling

ACADEMIC WORDS

DIRECTIONS
Choose the correct word for each definition below. Circle the letter of the correct answer.

7. _____: a set of questions designed to get information.
   A. bouquet
   B. survey
   C. tradition
   D. catalog

8. _____: happening in many places among many people or in many situations.
   A. plural
   B. wiggly
   C. ultimate
   D. widespread

9. _____: continue in the same way as before.
   A. maintain
   B. abridge
   C. prevent
   D. complain

10. _____: better, bigger, worse, etc., than others of the same kind.
    A. similar
    B. ultimate
    C. appreciate
    D. complete

11. _____: belief or custom that has existed for a long time.
    A. expedition
    B. inclination
    C. tradition
    D. politician

WORD STUDY

DIRECTIONS
Circle the letter of the word that forms a compound noun with the word in bold type.

12. **side**
    A. case
    B. hat
    C. walk
    D. desk

13. **tear**
    A. drop
    B. bow
    C. swell
    D. cry

14. **finger**
    A. thumb
    B. nail
    C. point
    D. write

15. **light**
    A. flicker
    B. heavy
    C. house
    D. glasses

16. **camp**
    A. forest
    B. bag
    C. spring
    D. ground

READING: "The Cowboy Era"

DIRECTIONS
Choose the word or phrase that best answers each question. Circle the letter of the correct answer.

17. Who brought cattle ranching to California?
    A. Mexican cowboys
    B. Native Americans
    C. Spanish missionaries
    D. Texas Longhorns

18. When Texas became a state in 1845, its economy depended on _____.
    A. grass and land
    B. cotton and cattle
    C. horses and sheep
    D. sharecropping and lariats

19. In the 1800s, cowboys participated in cattle drives which _____.
    A. allowed them to pass a required cowboy test
    B. moved cattle from Texas to the north and east
    C. involved loading cattle onto large steamer ships
    D. began in California and ended in Massachusetts

20. A cowboy wore clothing that was _____.
    A. stylish
    B. casual
    C. useful
    D. ancient

21. The cowboys were from different places, but they all _____.
    A. rode horses well
    B. grew up on farms
    C. liked to travel
    D. slept in one tent

22. For how many years were cowboys important in the U.S.?
    A. 10 years
    B. 20 years
    C. 50 years
    D. 100 years

23. Which two things caused the end of the cowboy era?
    A. Forest growth and wildlife
    B. Barbed wire and railroads
    C. Airplanes and automobiles
    D. Colleges and scholarships

DIRECTIONS

Choose the word or words that best complete each sentence. Circle the letter of the correct answer.

24. When I woke up, I _____ hear the birds gently chirping, so I smiled.
    A. might
    B. might not
    C. could
    D. shouldn't

25. It _____ be exciting to learn how to play guitar.
    A. have to
    B. might
    C. didn't
    D. mightn't

26. He always _____ make me laugh.
    A. couldn't
    B. might
    C. might not
    D. could

27. If you don't leave now, you _____ catch the bus.
    A. could
    B. might
    C. might not
    D. couldn't

28. Though she tried, Angela _____ find her keys.
    A. couldn't
    B. could
    C. might not
    D. might

29. They _____ visit the Grand Canyon on their next vacation.
    A. might
    B. couldn't
    C. might not
    D. could't

30. I _____ answer all of the questions because I had studied a lot.
    A. might
    B. could
    C. might not
    D. couldn't

STOP

UNIT 5

READING 4 TEST

LITERARY WORDS

DIRECTIONS
Choose the word that best completes each sentence. Circle the letter of the correct answer.

1. A way of describing something by exaggerating on purpose is _____.
   A. soliloquy
   B. hyperbole
   C. exclamation
   D. onomatopoeia

2. The use of words that imitate the sounds they represent is _____.
   A. soliloquy
   B. opportunity
   C. serendipity
   D. onomatopoeia

3. *The little bird twittered when the wind whooshed through the trees* is an example of _____.
   A. flamboyance
   B. hyperbole
   C. opposition
   D. onomatopoeia

4. *Yesterday, I caught a fish the size of a boat* is an example of _____.
   A. opposition
   B. exclamation
   C. hyperbole
   D. onomatopoeia

5. *The hot pan sizzled when she added oil* is an example of _____.
   A. ornamentation
   B. opposition
   C. onomatopoeia
   D. dialogue

6. *My hair is so shiny and golden that when I walk around town, people have to wear sunglasses* is an example of _____.
   A. hyperbole
   B. metaphor
   C. turbulence
   D. flamboyance

GO ON

DIRECTIONS
Choose the correct word for each definition below. Circle the letter of the correct answer.

DIRECTIONS
Read each item below. Circle the letter of the correct word to complete each sentence.

7. _____: not able to be seen.
   A. divisible
   B. visage
   C. unique
   D. invisible

8. _____: unusually good and special.
   A. rigid
   B. unique
   C. mellow
   D. fragile

9. _____: teach.
   A. instruct
   B. learn
   C. propose
   D. recall

10. _____: relationship in which two or more people work together.
    A. citizenship
    B. stewardship
    C. partnership
    D. dealership

11. _____: stiff and still.
    A. rigid
    B. strong
    C. unique
    D. invisible

12. _____: use something new or different instead of something else.
    A. instruct
    B. substitute
    C. prosecute
    D. differentiate

13. Have you seen _____ dog?
    A. there
    B. their
    C. they're
    D. tear

14. _____ your best friend?
    A. Who's
    B. Whose
    C. Who
    D. What

15. Look over _____!
    A. their
    B. they're
    C. there
    D. tear

16. She pushed the sofa _____ the side.
    A. two
    B. too
    C. to
    D. tow

17. _____ moving to Texas.
    A. Their
    B. They're
    C. Tear
    D. There

READING: From *Pecos Bill: The Greatest Cowboy of All Time*

DIRECTIONS
Choose the word or phrase that best completes each item or answers each question. Circle the letter of the correct answer.

18. Pecos Bill becomes separated from his family when _____.
    A. the animals kidnap him
    B. he jumps out to play with the animals
    C. the wagon hits a bump and he rolls out
    D. his brother pushes him out of the wagon

19. How does the child get the name "Pecos Bill"?
    A. His family names him after his great-grandfather Pecos.
    B. He takes the name to remember where he had been born.
    C. His family calls him that after the river where he was lost.
    D. The animals give him the name because of his appearance.

20. Who does Pecos Bill meet after becoming separated from his family?
    A. He meets a big, hungry Wolf.
    B. He meets a sharp, noisy Owl.
    C. He meets a sad, lonely Beaver.
    D. He meets a wise, old Coyote.

21. Cropear's teacher is _____.
    A. Grandy
    B. Pecos Bill
    C. Grizzly Bear
    D. Mountain Lion

22. Why does Grandy take Cropear to meet the other wild animals?
    A. He wants Cropear to leave.
    B. He wants to protect Cropear.
    C. He wants Cropear to hunt them.
    D. He wants Cropear to like him.

23. Cropear is the strongest, healthiest boy in the world because _____.
    A. he is part dog
    B. he smiles a lot
    C. he returns home
    D. he lives outdoors

GO ON

GRAMMAR

DIRECTIONS
Choose the word or words that best complete each sentence. Circle the letter of the correct answer.

24. Cheetahs are _____ than horses.
    - A. more speedy
    - B. speed
    - C. speediest
    - D. speedier

25. The kitchen is the _____ room in the house.
    - A. spacious
    - B. space
    - C. more spacious
    - D. most spacious

26. South America is _____ than North America.
    - A. heat
    - B. hotter
    - C. hottest
    - D. more hot

27. Many people are _____ of snakes than they are of bears.
    - A. most afraid
    - B. afraid
    - C. fright
    - D. more afraid

28. The _____ way to learn anything is to practice.
    - A. most
    - B. best
    - C. better
    - D. more

29. Your closet is _____ closet I've ever seen.
    - A. mess
    - B. the messiest
    - C. more messy
    - D. most messy

30. Is your English _____ this year than it was last year?
    - A. best
    - B. more
    - C. better
    - D. good

STOP

114   Unit 5 • Reading 4   Test   Grammar

Copyright © by Pearson Education, Inc.

UNIT 6 READING 1 TEST

LITERARY WORDS

DIRECTIONS
Choose the word that best completes each sentence. Circle the letter of the correct answer.

1. A female character in a story whose actions are inspiring or noble is a _____.
   A. heroine
   B. minstrel
   C. cherub
   D. heron

2. A fictional story told to explain natural events such as wind and rain is called a(n) _____.
   A. quote
   B. fable
   C. haiku
   D. myth

3. A male character in a story whose actions are inspiring or noble is a _____.
   A. twin
   B. lute
   C. hero
   D. halo

4. In the story, "Jack and the Beanstalk," Jack climbs the beanstalk and defeats the giant. Jack is the story's _____.
   A. hero
   B. myth
   C. person
   D. writer

5. *The sunlight on the water looked like diamonds. A strong wind carried the diamonds into the sky. That is why we can see stars at night,* is an example of a _____.
   A. novel
   B. hero
   C. myth
   D. song

6. The first line of a story begins, *Everyone but Melanie gave up.* Melanie is the story's _____.
   A. myth
   B. heroine
   C. person
   D. actress

GO ON

DIRECTIONS

Choose the correct word for each definition below. Circle the letter of the correct answer.

7. _____: make something as good as it was before.
   A. restore
   B. enforce
   C. reduce
   D. occupy

8. _____: function or part.
   A. goal
   B. role
   C. flag
   D. bran

9. _____: even though (something is known).
   A. for
   B. near
   C. over
   D. despite

10. _____: make someone do exactly what you want by deceiving or influencing him or her.
    A. stipulate
    B. relinquish
    C. delegate
    D. manipulate

11. _____: make someone obey.
    A. enforce
    B. approve
    C. assign
    D. outsource

12. _____: live, work, etc. in a place.
    A. enforce
    B. occupy
    C. restore
    D. manipulate

DIRECTIONS

Choose the antonym of the word in bold type. Circle the letter of the correct answer.

13. whisper
    A. mumble
    B. shout
    C. whistle
    D. breathe

14. weak
    A. strong
    B. messy
    C. smooth
    D. short

15. freeze
    A. toast
    B. burn
    C. chill
    D. cool

16. quickly
    A. loudly
    B. wildly
    C. slowly
    D. briskly

17. wild
    A. natural
    B. rough
    C. rowdy
    D. tame

READING: "How Glooskap Found the Summer" / "Persephone and the Pomegranate Seeds"

DIRECTIONS
Choose the word or phrase that best completes each item or answers each question. Circle the letter of the correct answer.

18. The Wawaniki people had a problem because _____.
    A. it was so hot that nothing could grow
    B. it was very cold and people began to die
    C. Winter put a charm on their leader Glooskap
    D. their leader Glooskap left and would not return

19. What does the myth "How Glooskap Found the Summer" explain?
    A. why the seasons change
    B. how grass and flowers grow
    C. why people need food to live
    D. how communities chose wise leaders

20. In "Persephone and the Pomegranate Seeds," Persephone's mother is the goddess of _____.
    A. agriculture
    B. geography
    C. astronomy
    D. temperature

21. Who takes Persephone to the underworld?
    A. Hermes
    B. Zeus
    C. Pluto
    D. Demeter

22. The twelve pomegranate seeds stand for _____.
    A. the twelve months
    B. the twelve seasons
    C. the twelve Greek gods
    D. the twelve grades in school

23. In both stories, which season is considered to be the best?
    A. fall
    B. winter
    C. spring
    D. summer

DIRECTIONS

Choose the word or words that best complete each sentence. Circle the letter of the correct answer.

24. Tomorrow, Pedro _____ buy a folder because he needs it for school.
    A. to
    B. had to
    C. has to
    D. have to

25. I _____ fix your broken bike if you want to ride it.
    A. can
    B. to
    C. won't
    D. has to

26. _____ you repeat the assignment, please?
    A. Do
    B. Could
    C. Must
    D. Have to

27. We _____ finish the job today because we're leaving tomorrow.
    A. could
    B. has to
    C. had to
    D. must

28. Lakshmi _____ buy boots yesterday because of the snowstorm.
    A. can
    B. may
    C. have to
    D. had to

29. We _____ go for a walk when the rain stops.
    A. has to
    B. did
    C. don't
    D. may

30. You _____ read the book after I finish reading it.
    A. did
    B. has to
    C. may
    D. had to

STOP

UNIT 6

READING 2 TEST

KEY WORDS

DIRECTIONS
Choose the word or words that best complete each sentence. Circle the letter of the correct answer.

1. A system of planets, moons, etc., that move around the sun is a(n) _____.
   A. sunspot
   B. ecosystem
   C. constellation
   D. solar system

2. A fact, condition, or happening that is unusual or difficult to understand is a
   _____.
   A. discovery
   B. juxtaposition
   C. phenomenon
   D. philosopher

3. One of the large groups of stars that make up the universe is called a(n)
   _____.
   A. gallon
   B. asteroid
   C. galaxy
   D. sentry

4. Facts or things that someone finds out about that weren't known before
   are _____.
   A. displays
   B. constellations
   C. discoveries
   D. conversations

5. Particular groups of stars named after something they seem to picture in an outline are called _____.
   A. formulations
   B. juxtapositions
   C. representatives
   D. constellations

6. A tube-shaped device used to make faraway objects look bigger and closer is a _____.
   A. television
   B. telescope
   C. phenomenon
   D. display

GO ON

DIRECTIONS

Choose the correct word for each definition below. Circle the letter of the correct answer.

7. _____: usual, expected, or obvious.
   A. spontaneous
   B. predictable
   C. legendary
   D. fascinating

8. _____: place or position.
   A. location
   B. diagram
   C. duration
   D. theory

9. _____: a person who studies life and what it means, how we should live, and what knowledge is.
   A. physician
   B. sociologist
   C. biologist
   D. philosopher

10. _____: idea that tries to explain something, but it may or may not be true.
    A. chasm
    B. theory
    C. debate
    D. question

11. _____: knew; recognized.
    A. sparked
    B. regretted
    C. identified
    D. intrigued

DIRECTIONS

Read each question below. Circle the letter of the correct answer.

12. Which word has a long *i* sound?
    A. win
    B. sip
    C. try
    D. quit

13. Which word has a short *i* sound?
    A. right
    B. swift
    C. kite
    D. reply

14. Which word has a long *i* sound?
    A. wife
    B. lift
    C. miss
    D. kick

15. Which word has a short *i* sound?
    A. cry
    B. high
    C. spin
    D. hike

16. Which word has a long *i* sound?
    A. big
    B. mill
    C. rim
    D. lie

17. Which word has a short *i* sound?
    A. sigh
    B. dig
    C. tie
    D. file

READING: "Early Astronomers"

DIRECTIONS

Choose the words or phrase that best completes each item or answers each question. Circle the letter of the correct answer.

18. How did ancient people use the stars?
    A. to travel through space
    B. to tell time and direction
    C. to avoid war and disease
    D. to light fires and cook food

19. What did the Maya develop that helped them know when to plant and harvest?
    A. a windmill
    B. a calendar
    C. a compass
    D. a thermometer

20. Ancient Greek astronomers _____.
    A. looked up at the stars in the night sky
    B. put a satellite in space and had it complete orbits
    C. used the stars to tell direction as they sailed the seas
    D. identified and recorded the location of stars in the sky

21. Al-Sufi located and identified more than _____.
    A. 20 planets
    B. 100 galaxies
    C. 500 patterns
    D. 1,000 stars

22. The first person to believe the sun was the center of the solar system was _____.
    A. Aristotle
    B. Galileo Galilei
    C. Johannes Kepler
    D. Nicholas Copernicus

23. Which scientist earned the name "the father of modern science"?
    A. Al-Sufi
    B. Galileo Galilei
    C. Johannes Kepler
    D. Nicolas Copernicus

GO ON

GRAMMAR

DIRECTIONS
Choose the word that best completes each sentence. Circle the letter of the correct answer.

24. All the students are _____ by the announcement.
    A. surprised
    B. surprising
    C. wondered
    D. wondering

25. Kerry thinks the homework is _____.
    A. remembered
    B. remembering
    C. confusing
    D. confused

26. Bicyclists often feel _____ when riding on busy streets.
    A. worrying
    B. worried
    C. traveling
    D. traveled

27. Don't be _____. Everyone makes mistakes sometimes.
    A. complained
    B. complaining
    C. embarrassed
    D. embarrassing

28. When you are tired, a soft chair looks _____.
    A. invited
    B. inviting
    C. warming
    D. warmed

29. Learning something new is always _____.
    A. interesting
    B. interested
    C. remembering
    D. remembered

30. My dog is _____ by loud noises.
    A. jumping
    B. jumped
    C. frightening
    D. frightened

READING 3 TEST

LITERARY WORDS

DIRECTIONS
Choose the words that best complete each sentence. Circle the letter of the correct answer.

1. A type of literature with imaginary events that involve science and technology is _____.
   A science fiction
   B. historical fiction
   C. technological fiction
   D. professional writing

2. Notes included in a play to describe how the work is supposed to be performed are _____.
   A. quarter notes
   B. action figures
   C. stage directions
   D. actors' instructions

3. *Kim and Jess hear a screeching sound. A glowing green object flies toward them. Now Kim is missing* is an example of _____.
   A. poetry
   B. science fiction
   C. fable
   D. mixed genre

4. *[knock at the door]* is an example of _____.
   A. dramatic flair
   B. quarter notes
   C. stage directions
   D. polite expression

5. *"Beware of creatures that have three eyes and eight arms. They are dangerous," the captain said,* is an example of _____.
   A. stage directions
   B. tragic drama
   C. realistic fiction
   D. science fiction

6. *[The lights go out]* is an example of _____.
   A. clear orders
   B. science fiction
   C. stage directions
   D. good guidelines

GO ON

ACADEMIC WORDS

DIRECTIONS

Choose the correct word for each definition. Circle the letter of the correct answer.

7. _____: able to be seen
   A. visible
   B. hidden
   C. modern
   D. contemporary

8. _____: easily noticed or understood
   A. abruptly
   B. gradually
   C. casually
   D. evidently

9. _____: something that happens
   A. version
   B. commotion
   C. occurrence
   D. circumstance

10. _____: discussing with other people
    A. conferring
    B. preventing
    C. obtaining
    D. commuting

11. _____: copy of something that has been slightly changed
    A. barrier
    B. version
    C. format
    D. vibration

WORD STUDY

DIRECTIONS

Choose the word that has the correct ending. Circle the letter of the correct answer.

12. A. laughible
    B. comfortible
    C. describible
    D. possible

13. A. horrable
    B. suitable
    C. visable
    D. sensable

14. A. inedable
    B. terrable
    C. available
    D. incredable

15. A. stoppible
    B. regrettible
    C. habitible
    D. incredible

16. A. questionable
    B. intangable
    C. sensable
    D. incredable

17. A. reasonible
    B. horrible
    C. laughible
    D. bearible

Name _____ Date _____

DIRECTIONS
Choose the phrase that best answers each question. Circle the letter of the correct answer.

18. What does Professor Pierson expect to see at the Wilmuth farm?
    A. a spaceship
    B. a thunderbolt
    C. a meteor
    D. an astronaut

19. Who is Dr. Gray?
    A. a professor at McGill University
    B. a medical doctor called to help sick people
    C. a famous astronomer from Princeton University
    D. a scientist from the National History Museum

20. The sound Mr. Wilmuth hears coming from the object sounds like _____.
    A a Fourth of July rocket hissing
    B. a band playing dancing music
    C. a group of people crying wildly
    D. a mirror shattering in many pieces

21. What does the crowd do when something comes out of the object?
    A. shouts and falls back
    B. moves toward the object
    C. watches and laughs
    D. photographs it

22. What comes out of the object?
    A. Piles of snakes slither out.
    B. Glistening bears climb out.
    C. Cinders shoot out of the object.
    D. Monsters with snake eyes climb out.

23. Carl Phillips' report ends because _____.
    A. the creatures return home
    B. the field catches fire
    C. he returns to the radio station
    D. everyone has tuned to another station

GO ON

DIRECTIONS
Choose the sentence that is correct. Circle the letter of the correct answer.

24. **A.** "I need to talk to you, Dad said,
    B. "I need to talk to you," Dad said.
    C. "I need to talk to you, Dad said,"
    D. "I need to talk to you Dad, said."

25. **A.** Rose said "I have two brothers"
    B. Rose, said, "I have two brothers."
    C. "Rose said I have two brothers"
    D. Rose said, "I have two brothers."

26. **A.** "Look out," cried Fred,
    B. "Look out cried Fred"
    C. "Look out," cried Fred.
    D. "Look out", cried, Fred.

27. **A.** Hanjae Said, "let's go to the mall and see a movie."
    B. Hanjae Said, "Let's go to the mall and see a movie."
    C. Hanjae said, "Let's go to the mall and see a movie."
    D. Hanjae said, "let's go to the mall and see a movie."

28. **A.** "My cousin wrote me a long letter," Barbara, said.
    B. "My cousin wrote me a long letter" Barbara, said.
    C. "My cousin wrote me a long letter." Barbara said.
    D. "My cousin wrote me a long letter," Barbara said.

29. **A.** Jane whispered, "I'll tell you a secret."
    B. "Jane whispered, I'll tell you a secret,"
    C. Jane "whispered, I'll tell you a secret,"
    D. Jane whispered, I'll tell you a secret,"

30. **A.** "in summer, we go to the beach," Lou said.
    B. "In summer, we go to the beach," Lou said.
    C. "In Summer, we go to the Beach," Lou said.
    D. "in summer, we go to the Beach," Lou said.

UNIT 6   READING 4 TEST

KEY WORDS

DIRECTIONS
Choose the word that best completes each sentence. Circle the letter of the correct answer.

1. An imaginary circle that divides Earth into the northern half and the southern half is the _____.
   A. equinox
   B. equator
   C. sphere
   D. elevator

2. One of the two halves of the Earth is a _____.
   A. stratosphere
   B. hemisphere
   C. atmosphere
   D. biosphere

3. The circular movement of something around a central point is called _____.
   A. rotation
   B. frustration
   C. declaration
   D. compensation

4. One of the two times in a year when night and day have equal lengths is the _____.
   A. axis
   B. solstice
   C. equator
   D. equinox

5. The imaginary line that the goes through the Earth's center from the North Pole to the South Pole is called the _____.
   A. belt
   B. peak
   C. axis
   D. vein

6. The longest or shortest day of the year is called the _____.
   A. crevice
   B. equinox
   C. axis
   D. solstice

GO ON

DIRECTIONS

Choose the correct word for each definition below. Circle the letter of the correct answer.

7. _____: limits that control the way something should be done
   A. observations
   B. positions
   C. reservations
   D. parameters

8. _____: solid round shape like a ball
   A. sphere
   B. scheme
   C. phase
   D. turret

9. _____: sends out signals
   A. revolves
   B. clashes
   C. outlines
   D. transmits

10. _____: two lines side by side and always the same distance apart
    A. linear
    B. parallel
    C. curved
    D. adjacent

11. _____: moves around a central point
    A. transmits
    B. placates
    C. revolves
    D. shimmers

12. _____: stage in a process
    A. sphere
    B. phase
    C. scheme
    D. parallel

DIRECTIONS

Choose the prefix that means the same as the boldfaced term. Circle the letter of the correct answer.

13. **earth**
    A. rota-
    B. kilo-
    C. astro-
    D. geo-

14. **equal, equally**
    A. rev-
    B. sol-
    C. equ-
    D. cycl-

15. **stars, outer space**
    A. astro-
    B. cycl-
    C. rev-
    D. kilo-

16. **circle, ring**
    A. geo-
    B. cycl-
    C. rota-
    D. rev-

17. **thousand**
    A. cycl-
    B. geo-
    C. rota-
    D. kilo-

READING: "Earth's Orbit"

DIRECTIONS
Choose the word or phrase that best completes each item or answers each question. Circle the letter of the correct answer.

18. Earth orbits the sun in _____.
    A. 24 days
    B. 350 days
    C. 365 days
    D. 390 days

19. What causes day and night?
    A. Earth's rotation on its axis
    B. the oval shape of Earth's orbit
    C. the summer and winter solstices
    D. the movement of the sun across the sky

20. The area near the equator is very hot because _____.
    A. it is always summer there
    B. soil absorbs heat faster there
    C. sunlight is spread over a greater area there
    D. sunlight travels to earth most directly there

21. Latitude is measured _____.
    A. in kilometers
    B. in solstices
    C. in degrees
    D. in gallons

22. In what month is the summer solstice?
    A. May
    B. June
    C. July
    D. August

23. Where is the noon sun during an equinox?
    A. directly overhead at the North Pole
    B. directly overhead at the South Pole
    C. directly overhead at Stonehenge
    D. directly overhead at the equator

GO ON

GRAMMAR

DIRECTIONS
Choose the phrase that gives the correct cause or effect. Circle the letter of the correct answer.

24. Laurent really wants a guitar. Therefore, _____.
    A. he is joining the band
    B. he is saving his money
    C. he has many friends
    D. he enjoys piano also

25. _____. Therefore, Bella arrived late.
    A. The movie was great
    B. She hung up the phone
    C. Her car broke down
    D. Her cat was sleeping

26. She wanted to take a picture, so _____.
    A. everyone smiled
    B. they walked home
    C. it became dark
    D. the lake was pretty

27. _____. As a result, the ground freezes.
    A. The flowers bloom
    B. The nights are cold
    C. The days are cloudy
    D. The river overflows

28. The cats are hungry, so _____.
    A. we read a book
    B. they take a nap
    C. we put out food
    D. we sit outside

29. _____. Therefore, the students went home.
    A. The bus is waiting
    B. Spring is lovely
    C. We invited a guest
    D. School ended for the day

30. Anna wakes up very early. As a result, _____.
    A. she feels sleepy at night
    B. her alarm clock broke
    C. the sun rises at 6 a.m.
    D. her sister sleeps late

B UNIT TESTS

UNIT 1

How does the natural world affect us?

UNIT TEST

LISTENING AND READING COMPREHENSION

DIRECTIONS
Listen to the passage "All about Parrots." Choose the best answer for each item. Circle the letter of the correct answer.

1. Parrots are very _____.
   A. old
   B. quiet
   C. smart
   D. hard-working

2. What can parrots do when they hear people talking?
   A. They can do your homework for you.
   B. They can write the words they hear.
   C. They can repeat the words they hear.
   D. They can laugh about what they hear.

3. What did a scientist teach a parrot to do?
   A. He taught a parrot to laugh and cry.
   B. He taught a parrot to cook and bake.
   C. He taught a parrot to think like a scientist.
   D. He taught a parrot to describe and count objects.

4. What can some parrots that live with dogs learn how to do?
   A. The parrots can learn to bark like a dog.
   B. The parrots can learn to turn lights on and off.
   C. The parrots can learn to take the dog for a walk.
   D. The parrots can learn to feed and bathe itself.

GO ON

DIRECTIONS

Read the questions about the reading selection from *Project Mulberry*. Choose the best answer for each item. Circle the letter of the correct answer.

5. Julia was glad that Patrick videotaped the caterpillar's actions because _____.
   A. she wants to watch the video many times
   B. she wants to show her teacher their hard work
   C. she does not know how to use the video camera
   D. she wants to send the videotape to a nature program

6. Julia is going to show the life cycle of the silkworm _____.
   A. by using photographs
   B. by using embroidery
   C. by using watercolors
   D. by using calligraphy

7. Julia is confused because she did not _____.
   A. get the book
   B. read the entire book
   C. know the project would take so long
   D. listen to her teacher in class

8. Patrick upset Julia when he told her that _____.
   A. they cannot make silk
   B. they do not make silk
   C. they have to kill the pupae to make silk
   D. he does not want to work on the project with her

DIRECTIONS

Read the questions about the reading "Ecosystems: The Systems of Nature." Choose the best answer for each item. Circle the letter of the correct answer.

9. An ant is _____.
   A. a species
   B. an organism
   C. a community
   D. an atmosphere

10. Only producers _____.
    A. eat other organisms
    B. make their own food
    C. consume certain fruits
    D. break down dead plants

11. The movement of food through a community is called _____.
    A. a food chain
    B. an organism
    C. a food circle
    D. a habitat

12. A population is members of the same species who _____.
    A. are the same age
    B. look exactly the same
    C. eat at the same time
    D. live in the same area

GO ON

Name _____ Date _____

DIRECTIONS

Read the questions about the reading selections "Ali, Child of the Desert" and "Desert Women". Choose the best answer for each item. Circle the letter of the correct answer.

13. Ali and his father are traveling to Rissani because they want _____.
    A. to sell their camels
    B. to find a new home
    C. to take their sheep to the mountains
    D. to avoid the yearly sandstorms

14. After Abdul leaves, Ali keeps the fire burning so _____.
    A. he can keep warm
    B. he can see the stars
    C. he can cook his food
    D. his father can find him

15. Abdul gives Ali _____.
    A. a musket and dates
    B. a rug and fresh water
    C. his turban and a camel
    D. firewood and ammunition

16. The poem "Desert Women" compares women who live in the desert to _____.
    A. fierce heat
    B. extreme cold
    C. cactus plants
    D. wailing braches

DIRECTIONS

Read the questions about the reading selection "Water and Living Things." Then, circle the letter next to the correct answer.

17. Most of the earth's water is _____.
    A. fresh
    B. salt
    C. rain
    D. bottled

18. The relationship between living things and water is that _____.
    A. only people need water to survive
    B. some living things need water, but other do not
    C. people need water more than plants do
    D. water is essential for all living things

19. The term for how water moves and changes forms over and over is _____.
    A. evaporation
    B. the water cycle
    C. condensation
    D. the water circle

20. The Chinese government is struggling to fix environmental problems by _____.
    A. buying water from other countries in the region
    B. forcing people to use less water and to recycle water
    C. turning salt water into fresh water in a big power plant
    D. moving water from the southern to the northern parts of the country

Unit 1 • Unit Test Listening and Reading Comprehension 135

DIRECTIONS

Choose the word or words that best complete each sentence. Circle the letter of the correct answer.

21. Plants make food using sunlight during a process called _____.
    A. philosophy
    B. organism
    C. photography
    D. photosynthesis

22. Animals that can have babies with each other belong to the same _____.
    A. organism
    B. ornament
    C. subculture
    D. species

23. The process in which water turns into water vapor and rises into the air is called _____.
    A. precipitation
    B. distribution
    C. evaporation
    D. condensation

24. The gases that surround the earth are called the _____.
    A. water cycle
    B. altitude
    C. atmosphere
    D. environment

25. Details of sight, sound, smell, taste, or touch are called _____.
    A. rhyming details
    B. surprising details
    C. sensory details
    D. imaginary details

26. Descriptive language that creates word pictures for readers is called _____.
    A. illusion
    B. imagery
    C. impression
    D. illustration

27. *The wind whistled in the trees* is an example of _____.
    A. legislation
    B. validation
    C. registration
    D. personification

28. *A cozy cottage set in a beautiful garden* is an example of _____.
    A. plot
    B. setting
    C. conflict
    D. character

Name _____ Date _____

DIRECTIONS
Choose the word or words that best complete each sentence. Circle the letter of the correct answer.

29. An amount out of every hundred is a _____.

    A. route
    B. process
    C. percent
    D. source

30. To have an effect on each other is to _____.

    A. imply
    B. fetch
    C. survive
    D. interact

31. To trust someone or something is to _____.

    A. rely
    B. fetch
    C. adapt
    D. survive

32. To change something so that it is the opposite of what it was before is to _____.

    A. relate
    B. react
    C. reverse
    D. resume

GO ON

DIRECTIONS

Choose the best answer for each item. Circle the letter of the correct answer.

33. The word *significant* means "important." Which word means "not important"?
    A. insignificant
    B. resignificant
    C. significantly
    D. signify

34. The verb *view* means "see." Which word means "to see again"?
    A. preview
    B. review
    C. viewpoint
    D. overview

35. The verb *work* means "toil." Which word means "do too much work"?
    A. worker
    B. rework
    C. workmanship
    D. overwork

DIRECTIONS

Read each item below. Circle the letter of the word that is spelled incorrectly.

39. A. background
    B. eye-lid
    C. grapefruit
    D. light bulb

40. A. checkmate
    B. waiting room
    C. earmuff
    D. motherinlaw

41. A. lip stick
    B. hummingbird
    C. motorcycle
    D. downstairs

DIRECTIONS

Read each sentence below. Circle the letter of the sentence with the underlined word that is spelled incorrectly.

36. A. She runs in all the <u>races</u>.
    B. I answer all the <u>questions</u>.
    C. He owns two <u>watches</u>.
    D. I have two <u>dictionarys</u>.

37. A. Some <u>caterpillars</u> make silk.
    B. All animals are <u>consumers</u>.
    C. She ate all the <u>ice cream</u>.
    D. He washed all the <u>dishs</u>.

38. A. She has pleasant <u>memories</u>.
    B. He tied his <u>shoelaces</u>.
    C. She put the <u>floweres</u> in a vase.
    D. Two <u>lights</u> flash in the dark.

DIRECTIONS

Choose the word with the same sound as the underlined part of the word in the box. Circle the letter of the correct answer.

42. | t<u>a</u>ke |
    A. back
    B. raise
    C. balance
    D. ham

43. | gr<u>ay</u> |
    A. lack
    B. fair
    C. mask
    D. payment

44. | st<u>a</u>ke |
    A. activity
    B. brain
    C. advantage
    D. metal

GRAMMAR

DIRECTIONS
Choose the word or words that best complete each sentence. Circle the letter of the correct answer.

45. Elena wears a _____ dress.
    A. green shiny silk
    B. silk green shiny
    C. shiny green silk
    D. silk shiny green

46. That is a _____ hat!
    A. big green wool
    B. wool big green
    C. wool green big
    D. green wool big

47. The movie was _____ I fell asleep.
    A. as boring that
    B. so boring that
    C. as boring as
    D. similarly

48. A habitat can be _____ an ocean.
    A. similarly
    B. as large that
    C. as large as
    D. so large that

49. In the sentence *Layla has many friends,* the predicate is _____.
    A. Layla has many
    B. Layla has
    C. has many friends
    D. many friends

50. In the sentence *David watches the sunset every evening,* the subject is _____.
    A. watches
    B. David
    C. sunset
    D. evening

51. Riva creates _____.
    A. pins lovely silver
    B. lovely pins silver
    C. silver lovely pins
    D. lovely silver pins

52. A cheetah can run _____ a car!
    A. as fast as
    B. so fast
    C. so fast that
    D. similarly that

53. The sun _____ in the west.
    A. were set
    B. setted
    C. sets
    D. setting

54. An autobiography is a true story. _____ an essay can be drawn from real life.
    A. Similarly,
    B. As true as,
    C. So true as,
    D. As similar as,

55. She _____ on my street.
    A. live
    B. living
    C. lives
    D. was lived

THE BIG QUESTION

How does the natural world affect us?

DIRECTIONS

Imagine that you visit a local or national park for a day with your class. On the lines below, write a journal entry in which you describe the park and your day there. Use images and details that appeal to the senses to help readers visualize how you feel, what you see, hear, and smell when you are in nature.

_____

_____

_____

_____

_____

_____

_____

_____

_____

_____

_____

_____

_____

_____

_____

_____

_____

_____

STOP

Name _____ Date _____

ORAL READING FLUENCY SCORE SHEET

All the members of one species in the same area are a   12

population. For example, all the frogs in a lake are a population. All the   26

pine trees in a forest are a population. All the people in a city, state, or   42

country are a population. Some populations do not stay in one place.   54

Monarch butterflies travel south each year from parts of western   64

Canada and the United States to Mexico. Some species of whales travel   76

around many oceans.   79

A community is all the populations that live together in one   90

place, such as all the plants and animals in a desert. In a community, the   105

different populations live close together, so they interact with one   115

another. One way populations interact in a community is by using the   127

same resources, such as food and shelter. In a desert, for example,   139

snakes, lizards, and spiders may all use rocks and holes for shelter.   151

They may eat insects, other animals, or their own kind of food.   163

Fluency Skill Assessed	Points Possible	Points Earned
Student reads with speed.	2	
Student reads with accuracy.	2	
Student reads with expression.	2	
Student reads with intonation.	2	
Student self-corrects.	2	

Total Score _____ / 10

Copyright © by Pearson Education, Inc.

ORAL READING FLUENCY

DIRECTIONS
Read the text below aloud for your teacher. Read with speed, accuracy, expression, and intonation.

All the members of one species in the same area are a population. For example, all the frogs in a lake are a population. All the pine trees in a forest are a population. All the people in a city, state, or country are a population. Some populations do not stay in one place. Monarch butterflies travel south each year from parts of western Canada and the United States to Mexico. Some species of whales travel around many oceans.

A community is all the populations that live together in one place, such as all the plants and animals in a desert. In a community, the different populations live close together, so they interact with one another. One way populations interact in a community is by using the same resources, such as food and shelter. In a desert, for example, snakes, lizards, and spiders may all use rocks and holes for shelter. They may eat insects, other animals, or their own kind of food.

UNIT 2

Where can a journey take you?
UNIT TEST

LISTENING AND READING COMPREHENSION

DIRECTIONS
Listen to the passage "A Rainbow without Rain." Choose the best answer for each item. Circle the letter of the correct answer.

1. Mrs. Bloom's flowers turned brown because they didn't get enough _____.
   A. sun
   B. shade
   C. rain
   D. soil

2. Mrs. Bloom's yard reminded Thomas of a(n) _____.
   A. painting
   B. rainbow
   C. island
   D. sunrise

3. You can tell from this passage that Thomas _____.
   A. likes Mrs. Bloom's yard
   B. does not like flowers
   C. wishes it would rain
   D. does not have a yard

4. Mrs. Bloom's new flowers will live because _____.
   A. they are much bigger
   B. they don't need much water
   C. they need a lot of sun
   D. they will stay inside

GO ON

DIRECTIONS

Read the questions about the reading selection from *Tales from the Odyssey.* Choose the best answer for each item. Circle the letter of the correct answer.

5. Odysseus and his men are trying to reach _____.
   A. Ithaca
   B. Egypt
   C. England
   D. Mount Olympus

6. The Greeks believe they have angered the gods because _____.
   A. they refused to eat the gods' flowers
   B. Greek warriors invaded Athena's temple
   C. Odysseus did not leave enough gold at the temple
   D. the warriors hurled thunderbolts at their enemies

7. When Odysseus is greeted by the islanders, they _____.
   A. are warm and friendly
   B. are suspicious and hostile
   C. tie up Odysseus and his men
   D. seem scared of him

8. The lotus blossoms are magical because they _____.
   A. make a man forget the past
   B. make a man no longer feel hungry
   C. help a man find his way home
   D. help a man row fast for a long time

DIRECTIONS

Read the questions about the reading "Early Explorers." Choose the best answer for each item. Circle the letter of the correct answer.

9. The main reason Phoenicians started to explore other lands was _____.
   A. to establish colonies
   B. to trade goods
   C. to learn languages
   D. to dig for gold

10. The Silk Road was created to _____.
    A. conduct trade between China and Europe
    B. open new lands for farmers and other settlers
    C. help the Chinese keep the secret of how to make silk
    D. prevent the Vikings from invading Europe and Asia

11. Europeans began sailing to China instead of taking the Silk Road because _____.
    A. the Silk Road was long and dangerous
    B. the King of Portugal commanded them to change
    C. the Europeans built ships that were like houses
    D. the Europeans wanted to stop in Portugal on the way

12. Christopher Columbus wanted to travel to _____.
    A. Spain
    B. America
    C. the East Indies
    D. the Caribbean

DIRECTIONS

Read the questions about the readings "Migrating Caribou" and "Magnets in Animals." Choose the best answer for each item. Circle the letter of the correct answer.

"Migrating Caribou"

13. The cold, treeless region of northern Asia, Europe, and North America is called the _____.
    A. South Pole
    B. Arctic tundra
    C. Migration Path
    D. Land of the Caribou

14. The caribou's favorite food is _____.
    A. mushrooms
    B. twigs
    C. grass
    D. lichen

"Magnets in Animals"

15. Some migrating animals may know their way because they _____.
    A. have learned the route
    B. use a built-in compass
    C. travel only during the daytime
    D. make very short journeys

16. In the winter, monarch butterflies _____.
    A. slowly die off
    B. turn into caterpillars
    C. migrate to warm places
    D. swim across the open sea

DIRECTIONS

Read the questions about the reading selection from *The Journal of Wong Ming-Chung.* Choose the best answer for each item. Circle the letter of the correct answer.

17. Wong Ming-Chung comes from _____.
    A. Headquarters in Chinatown
    B. San Francisco, California
    C. the area known as Four Districts in China
    D. the gold mines of the Golden Mountains

18. Wong Ming-Chung eats _____.
    A. dry biscuits and salted pork
    B. melons and big pots of stew
    C. only hard-boiled eggs and water
    D. excellent rice, vegetables, and meat

19. The first stone building in the area is built by _____.
    A. Chinese masons
    B. Wong Ming-Chung
    C. people born in America
    D. the ancient T'ang people

20. The wooden mansions are located _____.
    A. by the docks
    B. on Sacramento Street
    C. right in the middle of Chinatown
    D. on Stockton Street, above Chinatown

GO ON

VOCABULARY

DIRECTIONS
Choose the word or words that best complete each sentence. Circle the letter of the correct answer.

21. Open places or buildings with stalls where goods are sold are called _____.
    A. regions
    B. markets
    C. expeditions
    D. civilizations

22. A journey to an unknown place to find out more about it is an _____.
    A. extension
    B. expiration
    C. exploration
    D. extinction

23. Caribou travel in a large group called a _____.
    A. loom
    B. loft
    C. herd
    D. heir

24. Something that has the power to attract iron or steel is _____.
    A. magnetic
    B. apathetic
    C. mystic
    D. domestic

25. A sequence of connected events in a story is called a _____.
    A. plot
    B. simile
    C. point of view
    D. metaphor

26. A figure of speech that uses *like* or *as* to compare two things is a _____.
    A. metaphor
    B. plot
    C. point of view
    D. simile

27. *From my room, I saw the lightning strike the tree* is an example of _____.
    A. third-person point of view
    B. metaphor
    C. simile
    D. first-person point of view

28. *He is drowning in debt* is a _____.
    A. plot
    B. simile
    C. metaphor
    D. character

DIRECTIONS

Choose the word that best completes each sentence. Circle the letter of the correct answer.

29. To behave in a certain way because of what someone has done or said to you is to _____.
    A. react
    B. migrate
    C. transport
    D. emphasize

30. A large area is a _____.
    A. region
    B. season
    C. reply
    D. remedy

31. To move from one place to another is to _____.
    A. adjust
    B. expand
    C. migrate
    D. revive

32. Something that is existing or happening for a short time only is _____.
    A. honorary
    B. temporary
    C. luminary
    D. customary

DIRECTIONS

Choose the best answer for each item. Circle the letter of the correct answer.

33. Which root, when added before the letters *ory*, makes a word meaning "successful result of a contest"?
    A. *vid*
    B. *vis*
    C. *laps*
    D. *vict*

34. Which root, when added to the letters *com*, makes a word meaning "to order"?
    A. *vict*
    B. *vis*
    C. *mand*
    D. *vid*

35. Which root, when added before the letters *ible*, makes a word meaning "capable of being seen"?
    A. *vis*
    B. *laps*
    C. *vid*
    D. *vict*

GO ON

DIRECTIONS

Choose the correct noun form of each verb in bold type. Circle the letter of the correct answer.

36. **to explore**
     A. explorer
     B. explored
     C. exploratory
     D. has explored

37. **to sail**
     A. sale
     B. salient
     C. sailor
     D. sailed

38. **to translate**
     A. translator
     B. having translated
     C. translated
     D. transitory

DIRECTIONS

Read each sentence below. Identify the part of speech of each underlined word. Circle the letter of your answer.

39. Today's <u>math</u> lesson is on algebra.
     A. noun
     B. adjective
     C. verb
     D. pronoun

40. The <u>autumn</u> leaves smell musty.
     A. verb
     B. noun
     C. adjective
     D. pronoun

41. The telephone <u>cord</u> is tangled.
     A. adjective
     B. verb
     C. conjunction
     D. noun

DIRECTIONS

Choose the correct plural form of each word in bold type. Circle the letter of the correct answer.

42. **bunny**
     A. bunnies
     B. bunnys
     C. bunies
     D. bunnees

43. **copy**
     A. copyies
     B. copees
     C. copys
     D. copies

44. **pony**
     A. pony's
     B. ponny
     C. ponies
     D. ponnies

GRAMMAR

DIRECTIONS
Choose the past tense form of the verb that best completes each sentence. Circle the letter of the correct answer.

45. The farmer _____ a bucket of water.
    A. carryed   C. carrid
    B. carryd   D. carried

46. They _____ ready for the game.
    A. was   C. be
    B. were   D. went

DIRECTIONS
Choose the passive voice form of each sentence. Circle the letter of the correct answer.

47. Charles made soup.
    A. Charles soup made.
    B. Was made by Charles the soup.
    C. The soup was made by Charles.
    D. By Charles the soup having been made.

48. Traders sold cloth at the market.
    A. Cloth was sold at the market by traders.
    B. At the market, was sold by traders cloth.
    C. Cloth at the market sold.
    D. Cloth having sold at the market.

DIRECTIONS
Choose the word that best completes the sentence. Circle the letter of the correct answer.

49. A _____ washes grapes.
    A. cook careful
    B. careful cook
    C. carefully cook
    D. cook carefulled

50. Lena had a snack _____.
    A. until she got home from school
    B. upon she got home from school
    C. when she got home from school
    D. for she got home from school

51. Last week, Dad _____ he was well.
    A. saying
    B. says
    C. say
    D. said

52. In a month, my plant _____ six inches.
    A. growed
    B. grow
    C. grew
    D. growing

53. Juan learned _____ about fish.
    A. something interesting
    B. interesting something
    C. interesting
    D. intriguing something

54. They will cook dinner _____ they finish soccer practice.
    A. after
    B. which
    C. since
    D. for

DIRECTIONS
Choose the passive voice form of each sentence. Circle the letter of the correct answer.

55. Someone made a mistake.
    A. A mistake was made.
    B. Was made a mistake.
    C. It made a mistake.
    D. There was a mistake.

GO ON

THE BIG QUESTION
Where can a journey take you?

DIRECTIONS
Imagine you are traveling to a faraway place. Write a personal letter to a friend or family member. Tell what unexpected things have happened and how you reacted to each situation. Be sure to include details that help readers picture the journey. Write on the lines below.

_____

_____

_____

_____

_____

_____

_____

_____

_____

_____

_____

_____

_____

_____

_____

_____

_____

_____

ORAL READING FLUENCY SCORE SHEET

Not all exploration took place over rolling seas. The Silk Road	11
was a land route between Europe and Asia. It was used from around	24
500 B.C.E. until sea routes to China were opened up in about 1650. The	38
most important product traded along the Silk Road was silk. For	49
centuries the Chinese kept the secret of how to make silk from other	62
nations.	63
Along this road, trade was conducted between China and	72
Europe. Chinese merchants sent silk and spices to Europe over the	83
mountains and deserts of Asia. In return, gold, silver, and horses were	95
imported to China. The road was about 7,000 kilometers (4,300 mi) long	106
and very dangerous.	110
It passed through numerous kingdoms where rulers demanded	118
gifts from travelers. In addition, bandits would often pillage a traveling	129
camel train. Because of these dangers, the goods were passed from one	141
merchant to another, with no trader traveling for more than a few	153
hundred kilometers at a time.	158

Fluency Skill Assessed	Points Possible	Points Earned
Student reads with speed.	2	
Student reads with accuracy.	2	
Student reads with expression.	2	
Student reads with intonation.	2	
Student self-corrects.	2	

Total Score _____ / 10

Unit 2 • Unit Test   Oral Reading Fluency

DIRECTIONS
Read the text below aloud for your teacher. Read with speed, accuracy, expression, and intonation.

Not all exploration took place over rolling seas. The Silk Road was a land route between Europe and Asia. It was used from around 500 B.C.E. until sea routes to China were opened up in about 1650. The most important product traded along the Silk Road was silk. For centuries the Chinese kept the secret of how to make silk from other nations.

Along this road, trade was conducted between China and Europe. Chinese merchants sent silk and spices to Europe over the mountains and deserts of Asia. In return, gold, silver, and horses were imported to China. The road was about 7,000 kilometers (4,300 mi) long and very dangerous.

It passed through numerous kingdoms where rulers demanded gifts from travelers. In addition, bandits would often pillage a traveling camel train. Because of these dangers, the goods were passed from one merchant to another, with no trader traveling for more than a few hundred kilometers at a time.

UNIT 3 What defines success?

UNIT TEST

LISTENING AND READING COMPREHENSION

DIRECTIONS

Listen to the passage "A W-i-n-n-e-r!". Choose the best answer for each item. Circle the letter of the correct answer.

1. Evan O'Dorney won the Scripps National _____.
   A. Math Contest
   B. Science Fair
   C. Spelling Bee
   D. Music Competition

2. Evan thinks memorizing words is _____.
   A. fun
   B. easy
   C. difficult
   D. his favorite subject

3. Evan likes to _____.
   A. sing music
   B. write music
   C. conduct music
   D. perform music

4. Evan won a trophy, a large amount of money, and a _____.
   A. vacation
   B. video camera
   C. dictionary
   D. scholarship

GO ON

DIRECTIONS

Read the questions about the reading "Success Stories." Choose the best answer for each item. Circle the letter of the correct answer.

5. When Frida Kahlo was six years old, she _____.
   A. moved to Mexico City
   B. was in a bad bus accident
   C. got a serious illness called polio
   D. started painting self-portraits

6. Bill and Melinda Gates are trying to stop a disease called _____.
   A. malaria
   B. malaise
   C. polio
   D. bed nets

7. The villagers used the money Muhammad Yunus lent them to _____.
   A. travel to the US and earn a doctorate
   B. make bamboo stools and buy a cow
   C. start a bank and give loans to poor women
   D. buy textbooks and go to school

8. Mae Jamison brought small objects from West African countries into space because she wanted to _____.
   A. educate the other astronauts
   B. keep from feeling homesick
   C. show that space belongs to all nations
   D. test the effects of weightlessness

DIRECTIONS

Read the questions about the readings "An Interview with Naomi Shahib Nye" and "Making a Mosaic." Choose the best answer for each item. Circle the letter of the correct answer.

"An Interview with Naomi Shahib Nye"

9. Naomi Shihab Nye has lived in _____.
   A. Missouri, Texas, and Kansas
   B. Tel Aviv, Jerusalem, and Texas
   C. Texas, St. Louis, and New York City
   D. St. Louis, Jerusalem, and San Antonio

10. Naomi Shihab Nye tells young writers to _____.
    A. read a lot
    B. listen to music
    C. talk with others
    D. travel all over the world

"Making a Mosaic"

11. The title of this poem refers to _____.
    A. using a favorite plate for a party
    B. finding a plate that was in a shipwreck
    C. constructing a life from various experiences
    D. breaking a valuable plate while washing dishes

12. The person stands back to look at the mosaic to _____.
    A. admire it from far away
    B. look for a pattern
    C. look for mistakes
    D. ask a question

DIRECTIONS

Read the questions about the reading "The Marble Champ." Choose the best answer for each item. Circle the letter of the correct answer.

13. Lupe wins a small trophy from the mayor for _____.
    A. playing piano for senior citizens
    B. raising prize-winning flowers
    C. having excellent school attendance
    D. being the captain of the winning soccer team

14. Lupe practices playing marbles with _____.

    A. her mother
    B. her father
    C. her sister
    D. Miss Baseball Cap

15. While playing marbles in her backyard, Lupe beats _____.
    A. the neighborhood champ.
    B. her sister and her brother.
    C. her father's racquetball partner.
    D. her father and her mother.

16. Lupe pities her first opponent because _____.
    A. the girl does not have anyone to cheer for her
    B. the girl has clearly not practiced enough
    C. the girl has a small thumb and knuckles
    D. the girl has a broken thumb and wears mittens

DIRECTIONS

Read the questions about the reading "Students Win Robotics Competition." Choose the best answer for each item. Circle the letter of the correct answer.

17. Carl Hayden High School's challenge this year was to build _____.
    A. a robot to race other robots
    B. an underwater robot
    C. a robot to shoot soft foam balls through a hole
    D. a robot to help them with their homework

18. Carl Hayden High keeps winning the Chairman's Award because _____.
    A. they never finish first
    B. they always come in first place
    C. they build the best robot
    D. they encourage children to become interested in science and technology

19. A dangerous activity that a robot could perform today is _____.
    A. fighting wild fires
    B. arresting people
    C. jumping out of airplanes
    D. disarming bombs

20. The subjects that are the most important to engineers are _____.
    A. English and health
    B. art and physical education
    C. social studies and history
    D. science and math

DIRECTIONS

Choose the word or words that best complete each sentence. Circle the letter of the correct answer.

21. A spacecraft that is sent into orbit around the earth or the moon is a(n) _____.
    A. enterprise
    B. famine
    C. asterisk
    D. satellite

22. Money awards that are given to students to help pay for schooling are called _____.
    A. semesters
    B. robotics
    C. scholarships
    D. theories

23. The creation of a new idea, method, or invention is a(n) _____.
    A. innovation
    B. reputation
    C. corporation
    D. calculation

24. Ideas about how something works or why something happens are called _____.
    A. robotics
    B. theories
    C. projects
    D. labels

25. A figure of speech in which a comparison between two things continues for several lines is called a(n) _____.
    A. limited comparison
    B. extended metaphor
    C. stretched simile
    D. lengthy rhyme

26. A group of lines in a poem is called a _____.
    A. stanza
    B. simile
    C. rhyme
    D. cluster

27. *Vijay didn't know what he would find inside the tunnel. It was as dark as night. Then, he heard a strange noise* is an example of _____.
    A. repetition
    B. motivation
    C. suspense
    D. persona

28. *Louisa loved her little brother, so she played his favorite game* is an example of _____.
    A. a complex plot
    B. an extended metaphor
    C. suspense
    D. character motivation

DIRECTIONS

Choose the word that best completes each sentence. Circle the letter of the correct answer.

29. The thing that you think is most important is a(n) _____.
    A. priority
    B. objective
    C. event
    D. program

30. Exact and correct in every detail means _____.
    A. concise
    B. distinctive
    C. precise
    D. complicated

31. A goal that you are working hard to achieve is a(n) _____.
    A. lesson
    B. objective
    C. trophy
    D. recital

32. Knowledge or understanding is _____.
    A. aid
    B. commitment
    C. astonishment
    D. awareness

WORD STUDY

DIRECTIONS

Choose the best answer for each item. Circle the letter of the correct answer.

33. The prefix *re-* means "again." Which word means to "write again"?
    A. rewrite
    B. rework
    C. renew
    D. refund

34. The prefix *multi-* means "many." Which word means "many reasons"?
    A. repurpose
    B. multicultural
    C. multinational
    D. multipurpose

35. The prefix *under-* means "below." Which word means "not completed"?
    A. understood
    B. down under
    C. underdone
    D. undercook

GO ON

DIRECTIONS

Choose the correctly spelled form for each boldface word. Circle the letter of the correct answer.

36. **drop**
    A. droped
    B. droppd
    C. dropped
    D. dropted

37. **buy**
    A. buyying
    B. buying
    C. buing
    D. buiying

38. **call**
    A. called
    B. calld
    C. caled
    D. callded

DIRECTIONS

Choose the correct homophone for each boldface word. Circle the letter of the correct answer.

39. **there**
    A. theme
    B. there's
    C. their
    D. them

40. **pear**
    A. pare
    B. pearl
    C. peer
    D. prayer

41. **weather**
    A. weasel
    B. rather
    C. wear
    D. whether

DIRECTIONS

Choose the correct language of origin for each boldface word. Circle the letter of the correct answer.

42. **ecology**
    A. Spanish
    B. Italian
    C. Arabic
    D. German

43. **mammoth**
    A. Arabic
    B. Russian
    C. Italian
    D. Japanese

44. **protégé**
    A. German
    B. Chinese
    C. French
    D. Spanish

GRAMMAR

DIRECTIONS
Choose the word or words that best complete each sentence. Circle the letter of the correct answer.

45. We know the people _____.
   A. that next door
   B. who live next door
   C. they live next door
   D. that are next to

46. Reggie finished _____ the problem.
   A. solved
   B. solves
   C. to solve
   D. solving

47. Rico started _____ when he was in high school.
   A. jog
   B. jogs
   C. jogged
   D. jogging

48. Her teacher was pleased _____ her essay.
   A. to see
   B. seeing
   C. having seen
   D. see

49. _____ person has special abilities.
   A. All
   B. Every
   C. One of the
   D. Most

50. _____ Ken and Jiro will participate in the contest.
   A. Both
   B. Every
   C. All
   D. Most

51. Vincent van Gogh painted many pictures _____ were of flowers.
   A. that
   B. who
   C. whom
   D. where

52. The school was designed mainly for students _____ were interested in becoming doctors.
   A. when
   B. who
   C. whom
   D. which

53. _____ every day is a habit for my brother.
   A. Exercising
   B. Having exercised
   C. To be exercise
   D. Exercised

54. We go to the gym _____ we want to get fit.
   A. because
   B. for to
   C. why
   D. because of

55. My sister was thrilled _____ an A on her test.
   A. earn
   B. having earn
   C. earning
   D. to earn

GO ON

WRITING

THE BIG QUESTION
What defines success?

DIRECTIONS
Imagine that you are old and you have led a successful life. Write an expository paragraph about your life. Describe specific things that you did to make your life a success. Write on the lines below.

_____

_____

_____

_____

_____

_____

_____

_____

_____

_____

_____

_____

_____

_____

_____

_____

_____

_____

ORAL READING FLUENCY SCORE SHEET

Mae Jemison was born in 1956 in Decatur, Alabama. She grew up	11
in Chicago, Illinois. When she was growing up, Jemison watched	22
spaceflights on television. After college, she went to medical school	32
and also took graduate courses in engineering. What she really wanted,	43
however, was to be a space traveler. In 1987, Dr. Jemison was one of	57
fifteen people, out of almost 2,000 applicants, chosen for NASA's	67
astronaut training program.	70
On September 12, 1992, Dr. Jemison and six other astronauts went	80
into orbit aboard the space shuttle *Endeavour*. Dr. Jemison was the first	91
African-American female astronaut. During her seven-day flight, she	99
did experiments to understand the effects of weightlessness. She carried	109
with her several small objects from West African countries. She did this	120
to show her belief that space belongs to all nations.	133
Dr. Jemison is currently a professor of community and family	143
medicine at Dartmouth College, New Hampshire. She is active	152
worldwide in science literacy and sustainable development.	159

Fluency Skill Assessed	Points Possible	Points Earned
Student reads with speed.	2	
Student reads with accuracy.	2	
Student reads with expression.	2	
Student reads with intonation.	2	
Student self-corrects.	2	

Total Score _____ / 10

DIRECTIONS
Read the text below aloud for your teacher. Read with speed, accuracy, expression, and intonation.

Mae Jemison was born in 1956 in Decatur, Alabama. She grew up in Chicago, Illinois. When she was growing up, Jemison watched spaceflights on television. After college, she went to medical school and also took graduate courses in engineering. What she really wanted, however, was to be a space traveler. In 1987, Dr. Jemison was one of fifteen people, out of almost 2,000 applicants, chosen for NASA's astronaut training program.

On September 12, 1992, Dr. Jemison and six other astronauts went into orbit aboard the space shuttle *Endeavour*. Dr. Jemison was the first African-American female astronaut. During her seven-day flight, she did experiments to understand the effects of weightlessness. She carried with her several small objects from West African countries. She did this to show her belief that space belongs to all nations.

Dr. Jemison is currently a professor of community and family medicine at Dartmouth College, New Hampshire. She is active worldwide in science literacy and sustainable development.

UNIT 4

Can we see change as it happens?

UNIT TEST

LISTENING AND READING COMPREHENSION

DIRECTIONS
Listen to the passage "Bored Bailey." Choose the best answer for each item. Circle the letter of the correct answer.

1. When the story opens, Bailey feels
   _____.
   A. angry
   B. hungry
   C. tired
   D. bored

2. Bailey is _____.
   A. a dog
   B. a young boy
   C. Marcus's brother
   D. a teenage boy

3. Marcus takes Bailey to the beach because he wants _____.
   A. Bailey to learn to swim
   B. Bailey to be happy
   C. Bailey to learn play ball
   D. to punish Bailey for ripping up newspapers

4. In the end, Bailey feels happy because _____.
   A. he ate delicious food
   B. he made Marcus happy
   C. he had fun and played all day
   D. he learned important new skills

GO ON

DIRECTIONS

Read the questions about the reading "Changing Earth." Choose the best answer for each item. Circle the letter of the correct answer.

5. In the last 200 years, the earth's population has _____.
   A. grown a little
   B. grown a lot
   C. decreased a little
   D. decreased a lot

6. The earth's resources are _____.
   A. limited
   B. renewable
   C. everlasting
   D. finished

7. Scientists are changing the food supply by using _____.
   A. genuine manipulation
   B. genetic engineering
   C. geological surveys
   D. generous planting

8. How are solar-powered cars and hydrogen-powered cars different?
   A. Solar-powered cars must stay outside in the sun, while hydrogen-powered cars can be stored in a dark garage because they use gas.
   B. Solar-powered cars change energy from the sun into oil, while hydrogen-powered cars combine power from oxygen and gas to produce power.
   C. Solar-powered cars change energy from the sun into gas, while hydrogen-powered cars combine the sun and oil.
   D. Solar-powered cars change energy from the sun into electricity, while hydrogen-powered cars use fuel cells that combine two gases.

DIRECTIONS

Read the questions about the reading "The Intersection." Choose the best answer for each item. Circle the letter of the correct answer.

9. The second letter was written in _____.
   A. 1800
   B. 1950
   C. 1900
   D. 2000

10. Jason Winthrop wrote the first letter because he wanted people to _____.
    A. visit him
    B. buy cars
    C. slow down
    D. clean up

11. Over the years, the city became _____.
    A. larger
    B. famous
    C. smaller
    D. run-down

12. Jason Winthrop III doesn't want to sell his house because _____.
    A. it is a very fancy wooden house and everyone in town admires it
    B. people will not pay the money that he feels the house is worth
    C. he has set up a business in the house and does not want to relocate it
    D. the house has been in his family a long time and he does not want to move

Name _____ Date _____

DIRECTIONS
Read the questions about the reading selections from *Through My Eyes*, "Harlem Then and Now," *Tar Beach,* and "Dreams." Choose the best answer for each item. Circle the letter of the correct answer.

Through My Eyes

13. In 1954, the Supreme Court _____.
 A. outlawed Mardi Gras in New Orleans
 B. ordered the end of school segregation
 C. built new schools for African-American students in the South
 D. established the system of federal marshals

14. Ruby's parents were persuaded to send Ruby to an all-white school by _____.
 A. the NAACP
 B. the neighbors
 C. Ruby's teacher
 D. a federal marshal

15. Ruby's mother wanted her to attend William Frantz Public School because she wanted her to _____.
 A. challenge the federal law
 B. obey the NAACP's wishes
 C. take more important tests
 D. receive the best education possible

16. US federal marshals took Ruby to school because _____.
 A. her father was a famous movie actor
 B. she was part of a Mardi Gras parade
 C. people were celebrating school integration
 D. some people were against school integration

"Harlem: Then and Now"

17. Baldwin wants the tenements rebuilt because _____.
 A. they cost too much to maintain
 B. they do not leave enough room for children to play
 C. they are dangerous, especially if a fire breaks out
 D. they take up space that could be used for mansions

18. Baldwin's message is _____.
 A. Harlem has not changed much in 400 years
 B. Harlem once had many fine mansions, now torn down
 C. Harlem should return to its roots as a farming community
 D. Harlem has a rich history, but there is room for improvement

Tar Beach

19. In this story quilt, the girl imagines she's flying because she wants to _____.
 A. study migrating birds and butterflies
 B. be free to go anywhere she wants
 C. become an airline pilot and travel a lot
 D. visit a relative who lives very far away

"Dreams"

20. In this poem, Hughes tells readers to _____.
 A. talk about their dreams
 B. ignore their dreams
 C. stop dreaming so much
 D. not put off their dreams

GO ON

DIRECTIONS
Choose the word or words that best completes each sentence. Circle the letter of the correct answer.

21. Fuels that were formed from the remains of plants and animals from long ago are called _____.
    A. firm fuels
    B. solar power
    C. fancy fuels
    D. fossil fuels

22. Something that is a mixture of two or more things is a(n) _____.
    A. hybrid
    B. incident
    C. hyphen
    D. consequence

23. Unfair treatment of people based on their race is called _____.
    A. reflection
    B. racism
    C. radiation
    D. segregation

24. Judges in a court of law are sometimes called _____.
    A. justices
    B. troops
    C. lawyers
    D. fedoras

25. A hint or a clue in a story about what will happen later on is called _____.
    A. backing
    B. chattering
    C. foreshadowing
    D. shadowboxing

26. *Marlena said, "You're not listening to me at all." Kira screamed, "Yes, I am!"* is an example of _____.
    A. conflict
    B. convict
    C. rhyme
    D. verdict

27. The central idea, or message, of a work of literature is called the _____.
    A. rhyme
    B. cornice
    C. theme
    D. dialect

28. *One, two, buckle her shoe.* is an example of a _____.
    A. conflict
    B. theme
    C. rhyme
    D. reference

GO ON

DIRECTIONS
Choose the word that best completes each sentence. Circle the letter of the correct answer.

29. An official rule or order is a _____.
   A. regulation
   B. generation
   C. conversation
   D. dialogue

30. Something that happens as a result of a particular action is a(n) _____.
   A. incident
   B. evaluation
   C. circumstance
   D. consequence

31. Something that is easy to understand or obvious is _____.
   A. enormous
   B. apparent
   C. reluctant
   D. attainable

32. One part of something is a _____.
   A. section
   B. alternative
   C. regulation
   D. community

GO ON

DIRECTIONS

Read each question below and find the correct answer. Circle the letter of the correct answer.

33. Which is an adjective form of *transport*?
    A. transporter
    B. multitransport
    C. transported
    D. transportation

34. Which is a noun form of *insert*?
    A. insertion
    B. inserted
    C. inserting
    D. inset

35. Which is a noun form of *improve*?
    A. improvement
    B. improved
    C. improvisation
    D. improbable

36. Which is a synonym for *hot*?
    A. chilly
    B. aloof
    C. burning
    D. vacant

37. Which is a synonym for *slow*?
    A. spirited
    B. sluggish
    C. lavish
    D. sparkling

38. Which is a synonym for *hurt*?
    A. injured
    B. tired
    C. hungry
    D. delighted

DIRECTIONS

Read each question below and find the correct answer. Circle the letter of the correct answer.

39. Which word or words should be capitalized?
    A. list
    B. city
    C. famous award
    D. nobel peace prize

40. Which word should be capitalized?
    A. cheese
    B. stove
    C. french
    D. shoes

41. Which word or words should be capitalized?
    A. favorite teacher
    B. best friend
    C. dr. sanchez
    D. soccer team

42. Which word has a long *e* sound?
    A. bet
    B. dye
    C. tea
    D. den

43. Which word has a long *e* sound?
    A. separate
    B. leopard
    C. tender
    D. reason

44. Which word has a long *e* sound?
    A. letter
    B. fennel
    C. seed
    D. except

GRAMMAR

DIRECTIONS
Choose the word or words that best complete each sentence. Circle the letter of the correct answer.

45. Carmen and Rocco _____ to the store.
    A. has drove
    B. has drived
    C. have drove
    D. have driven

46. Since they live very far away, they _____ to visit us.
    A. won't come probably
    B. will come probably
    C. will probably come
    D. probably won't come

47. I didn't go to the party last year, _____ I plan to go this year.
    A. when
    B. but
    C. or
    D. none of the above

48. I will arrive there by train _____ by plane.
    A. and
    B. but
    C. or
    D. none of the above

49. Will you let me borrow _____ favorite book?
    A. you
    B. your
    C. yours
    D. you's

50. Don't sit on that chair! One of _____ legs is broken.
    A. its
    B. their
    C. it's
    D. his

51. The store _____ problems keeping the popular book in stock.
    A. has had
    B. have
    C. having
    D. to have

52. She doesn't like spinach, _____ she will eat it to be polite.
    A. and
    B. but
    C. or
    D. none of the above

53. The insects _____ eat all the tomatoes in her garden.
    A. will
    B. be
    C. has
    D. have

54. _____ not start until this evening.
    A. Probably the storm
    B. The storm maybe
    C. The storm probably
    D. Maybe the storm will

55. She has to go to the grocery store _____ the dry cleaners.
    A. and
    B. but
    C. so
    D. none of the above

THE BIG QUESTION

Can we see change as it happens?

DIRECTIONS

Think about a place you know well. How has it changed? Do you like the changes?
Write a letter to the editor of the local newspaper. Persuade the readers to make
some changes that you would like to see. Be sure to include facts, details, and
examples to support your argument. Write on the lines below.

_____

_____

_____

_____

_____

_____

_____

_____

_____

_____

_____

_____

_____

_____

_____

_____

_____

_____

_____

STOP

Name _____ Date _____

Scientists are looking for new ways to power cars and other	11
vehicles, such as by using batteries, solar power, and fuel cells. In an	24
all-electric car, a large, heavy battery stores the electric energy that	35
powers the car. When the battery runs low, the driver must recharge it	48
by plugging it into a special electric outlet. Recharging the battery takes	60
much longer than refilling a gasoline tank. Even so, electricity is a	72
relatively clean source of energy for cars, so this extra effort benefits	84
the environment.	86
Some car manufacturers have developed hybrid cars. These cars	95
run on a combination of electricity and gasoline. Their batteries are	106
small and can be recharged by the car's small gasoline engine while the	119
car is being driven.	123
Scientists are also experimenting with solar-powered cars and	131
hydrogen-powered cars. Solar-powered cars use solar cells to change	140
energy from the sun into electricity. Hydrogen-powered cars use fuel	150
cells that combine two gases—hydrogen and oxygen—to produce	160
electricity. Solar and fuel cells are clean energy sources.	169

Fluency Skill Assessed	Points Possible	Points Earned
Student reads with speed.	2	
Student reads with accuracy.	2	
Student reads with expression.	2	
Student reads with intonation.	2	
Student self-corrects.	2	

Total Score _____ / 10

Unit 4 • Unit Test   Oral Reading Fluency

DIRECTIONS
Read the text below aloud for your teacher. Read with speed, accuracy, expression, and intonation.

Scientists are looking for new ways to power cars and other vehicles, such as by using batteries, solar power, and fuel cells. In an all-electric car, a large, heavy battery stores the electric energy that powers the car. When the battery runs low, the driver must recharge it by plugging it into a special electric outlet. Recharging the battery takes much longer than refilling a gasoline tank. Even so, electricity is a relatively clean source of energy for cars, so this extra effort benefits the environment.

Some car manufacturers have developed hybrid cars. These cars run on a combination of electricity and gasoline. Their batteries are small and can be recharged by the car's small gasoline engine while the car is being driven.

Scientists are also experimenting with solar-powered cars and hydrogen-powered cars. Solar-powered cars use solar cells to change energy from the sun into electricity. Hydrogen-powered cars use fuel cells that combine two gases—hydrogen and oxygen—to produce electricity. Solar and fuel cells are clean energy sources.

UNIT 5

Why do we explore new frontiers?

UNIT TEST

LISTENING AND READING COMPREHENSION

DIRECTIONS

Listen to the passage "Space, the Final Frontier." Then choose the best answer for each item. Circle the letter of the correct answer.

1. According to the passage, what are most people surprised to learn about outer space?
    A. that space is not empty
    B. that space has major planets
    C. that comets come from asteroids
    D. that space has planets and moons

2. How are asteroids different from comets?
    A. Asteroids don't move, but comets do.
    B. All asteroids are much larger than comets.
    C. Asteroids don't have tails, but comets do.
    D. Asteroids are made of rock, but comets are all ice.

3. Asteroids are similar to planets because _____.
    A. both asteroids and planets can sustain life
    B. all asteroids and planets have been named
    C. both asteroids and planets can have moons
    D. all asteroids and planets are roughly the same size

4. The asteroid belt is located _____.
    A. in the sun
    B. near the Galileo
    C. next to asteroid Ida
    D. between Mars and Jupiter

GO ON

DIRECTIONS

Read the questions about the readings from *River to Tomorrow*, "River Song," and "Morning Prayer Song." Choose the best answer for each item. Circle the letter of the correct answer.

River to Tomorrow

5. Where does Sacagawea go in this story?
   A. to the Atlantic Ocean
   B. to the Five Tribes
   C. to the Pacific
   D. to visit the American explorers

6. The trip up the river is best described as _____.
   A. a lot of fun
   B. extremely easy
   C. not that difficult
   D. very difficult

"River Song"

7. What is the singer singing about in this poem?
   A. The singer bemoans life's sorrows.
   B. The singer describes the value of memories.
   C. The singer tells about the world's rivers.
   D. The singer praises the tribe's children.

"Morning Prayer Song"

8. The speaker concludes that _____.
   A. all is well
   B. things are best in the north
   C. it is important to get up early
   D. children should listen to their grandparents

DIRECTIONS

Read the questions about the reading "Maps and Compasses." Choose the best answer for each item. Circle the letter of the correct answer.

9. On a relief map you can see if a place _____.
   A. has wet or dry climate
   B. has forests, farms, and deserts
   C. has plains, hills, and mountains
   D. has a large or a small population

10. The compass points _____.
    A. to the sun
    B. to your home
    C. to the North Pole
    D. to the Pacific Ocean

11. A compass tells you _____.
    A. what time zone you are in
    B. what direction you are facing
    C. where the closest water source is
    D. how long it will take to reach home

12. What do you need to make a simple compass?
    A. You need a scale, key, cork cut in half, and a scissors.
    B. You need a needle, round card, lodestone, and relief map.
    C. You need a set of colored pencils, map, and container filled with water.
    D. You need a needle, magnet, small cork, and container filled with water.

Name _____ Date _____

DIRECTIONS
Read the questions about the reading "The Cowboy Era." Choose the best answer for each item. Circle the letter of the correct answer.

13. Who brought the first domesticated cows and horses to Mexico?
    A. Texas ranchers brought them.
    B. Native Americans brought them.
    C. Former slaves brought them.
    D. Spanish settlers brought them.

14. Cattle ranching became important because _____.
    A. wild cows were damaging the crops
    B. Americans liked to eat beef
    C. cattle helped farmers gather cotton
    D. cowboys found work on ranches

15. Why was cowboy life dangerous?
    A. Cowboys did not have the proper clothing for the job.
    B. Cowboys tried to steal cattle and often got caught.
    C. Cattle drives were difficult and sometimes dangerous.
    D. The price of cattle often dropped, so cowboys lost their jobs.

16. The cowboy era lasted _____.
    A. five years
    B. fifteen years
    C. twenty years
    D. fifty years

DIRECTIONS
Read the questions about the reading from *Pecos Bill: The Greatest Cowboy of All Time.* Choose the best answer for each item. Circle the letter of the correct answer.

17. Pecos Bill has such an unusual childhood because _____.
    A. his family lives in the wild west
    B. he is raised by the Coyotes
    C. he has eight or ten older brothers and sisters
    D. his parents let him have wild animals as pets

18. How do Pecos Bill and his family get separated?
    A. The wagon hits a bump and Pecos Bill rolls out.
    B. Wild animals steal Pecos Bill because they want to eat him.
    C. Pecos Bill jumps out of the wagon to play with the animals.
    D. Pecos Bill's brothers and sisters push him out of the wagon.

19. Who is Grandy?
    A. Grandy is the leader of the Coyotes.
    B. Grandy is Pecos Bill's kind grandmother.
    C. Grandy is Pecos Bill's brother.
    D. Grandy is the old horse that pulls the wagon.

20. The two animals that refuse to help Pecos Bill are _____.
    A. Skunk and Porcupine
    B. Cropear and Bull Rattlesnake
    C. Mountain Lion and Grizzly Bear
    D. Wouser and the Bull Rattlesnake

GO ON ➡

VOCABULARY

DIRECTIONS
Choose the word or words that best complete each sentence. Circle the letter of the correct answer.

21. To measure distance between a starting point and a place on a map you would use a _____.
A. relief
B. scribe
C. track
D. scale

22. What is the measurement of height above sea level called?
A. It is called astronomy.
B. It is called elevation.
C. It is called wavelength.
D. It is called barometer.

23. People who go to live in a new country, colony, or region are called _____.
A. peddlers
B. drifters
C. settlers
D. sharecroppers

24. Freedom from being controlled by other people or governments is called _____.
A. banishment
B. elevation
C. defense
D. independence

25. A conversation between characters is called _____.
A. dialogue
B. analogy
C. interlude
D. prologue

26. A way of describing something by exaggerating on purpose is called _____.
A. jocularity
B. excursion
C. hyperbole
D. synergy

27. *As Cecil looked at the picture, he thought about his kind grandmother. He remembered how she had made him a delicious cake for his seventh birthday so many years ago* is an example of _____.
A. fallout
B. crossroad
C. seesaw
D. flashback

28. *The bee buzzed and buzzed* is an example of _____.
A. flashback
B. onomatopoeia
C. demonstration
D. glockenspiel

DIRECTIONS
Choose the word that best completes each sentence. Circle the letter of the correct answer.

29. Something you want to do in the future is a _____.
    A. chart
    B. goal
    C. grate
    D. patrol

30. If something is next to something else, it is _____.
    A. adjacent
    B. diagonal
    C. central
    D. competent

31. A set of questions designed to get information is called a _____.
    A. essay
    B. label
    C. display
    D. survey

32. If something can't be seen, it is _____.
    A. rigid
    B. erasable
    C. invisible
    D. minimal

GO ON

WORD STUDY

DIRECTIONS

Choose a synonym for each boldfaced word. Circle the letter of the correct answer.

33. **late**
    A. rate
    B. early
    C. tardy
    D. light

34. **repair**
    A. fix
    B. lick
    C. stop
    D. break

35. **cold**
    A. humid
    B. chilly
    C. muggy
    D. cloudy

DIRECTIONS

Circle the letter of the word that forms a compound noun with the boldface word.

39. **back**
    A. tan
    B. stereo
    C. ground
    D. sweater

40. **candle**
    A. night
    B. light
    C. smell
    D. box

41. **home**
    A. burn
    B. lift
    C. sleep
    D. work

DIRECTIONS

Read each question below. Circle the letter of the correct answer.

36. Which word has a long *e* sound?
    A. weight
    B. metro
    C. chief
    D. wedge

37. Which word has a long *a* sound?
    A. sleigh
    B. fiery
    C. either
    D. chief

38. Which word has a long *e* sound?
    A. legend
    B. siege
    C. weight
    D. vestige

DIRECTIONS

Choose the correct word or words to complete each sentence. Circle the letter of the correct answer.

42. Ride _____ the corner.
    A. to
    B. two
    C. toe
    D. too

43. _____ good singers.
    A. They're
    B. There
    C. Here
    D. Their

44. _____ shoes are these?
    A. Who's
    B. Whose
    C. Hose
    D. Who is

GO ON

Name _____ Date _____

DIRECTIONS
Choose the word or words that best complete each sentence. Circle the letter of the correct answer.

45. Before she _____ outside, the school bus _____.
    A. will walk/left
    B. had walked/will leave
    C. walked/had left
    D. walks/had left

46. _____ off the light before you leave the room, please.
    A. Change
    B. Switch
    C. Pull
    D. Close

47. Carmen _____ whistle ever since she was five.
    A. might not
    B. might
    C. could not
    D. could

48. I _____ go because it is too expensive.
    A. might
    B. might not
    C. could
    D. can

49. Henry is _____ boy on the team.
    A. the laziest
    B. more lazy
    C. lazier
    D. most lazy

50. Autumn is _____ than spring.
    A. pleasanter
    B. most pleasant
    C. more pleasant
    D. pleasantest

51. By the time he _____ the speech, the other students _____ asleep!
    A. finished/ fallen
    B. had finished/ fallen
    C. had finished/ will fall
    D. finished/ had fallen

52. _____ me the plate, please.
    A. Give
    B. Gave
    C. You giving
    D. Giving

53. _____ the books on the table.
    A. Placing
    B. Place
    C. To place
    D. Having placed

54. Some cats _____ hurt themselves climbing trees, but others won't.
    A. might
    B. have to
    C. should
    D. could have

55. This movie is _____ than the other one we saw.
    A. sadder
    B. more sadder
    C. most sadder
    D. the saddest

THE BIG QUESTION
Why do we explore new frontiers?

DIRECTIONS
Think of the first time you visited a new place. Why did you visit this place? Write a letter to someone who is planning to visit the same place. Tell about some of the good things about the place. Then give instructions for places to play and things to see and do. Write on the lines below.

_____

_____

_____

_____

_____

_____

_____

_____

_____

_____

_____

_____

_____

_____

_____

_____

_____

_____

_____

_____

STOP

Name _____ Date _____

ORAL READING FLUENCY SCORE SHEET

Some days were scorching hot, and some nights were freezing	10
cold. Cowboys wore practical clothes to help them withstand these	20
temperatures.	21
Cowboy hats had to be strong and long lasting. On hot days, the high	34
top part of the hat kept the head cool, while the broad brim shaded the	49
eyes and neck. On rainy or snowy days, the hats worked as	62
umbrellas. The hats also protected cowboys from thorns and	71
low-hanging branches. Cowboys even used them to carry water, to fan	82
or put out fires, and as pillows.	89
The cowboys' other clothing was also practical. Their shirts and	99
pants were made of strong material. They lasted a long time and	111
protected the cowboys' skin. When it was dusty, cowboys covered their	122
noses and mouths with the bandannas they wore around their necks.	133
When riding horses, cowboys used their boot heels to prevent	143
their feet from slipping out of the stirrups. When roping cattle, the	155
cowboys could dig their boot heels into the ground.	164

Fluency Skill Assessed	Points Possible	Points Earned
Student reads with speed.	2	
Student reads with accuracy.	2	
Student reads with expression.	2	
Student reads with intonation.	2	
Student self-corrects.	2	

Total Score _____ / 10

Unit 5 • Unit Test   Oral Reading Fluency

DIRECTIONS

Read the text below aloud for your teacher. Read with speed, accuracy, expression, and intonation.

Some days were scorching hot, and some nights were freezing cold. Cowboys wore practical clothes to help them withstand these temperatures.

Cowboy hats had to be strong and long lasting. On hot days, the high top part of the hat kept the head cool, while the broad brim shaded the eyes and neck. On rainy or snowy days, the hats worked as umbrellas. The hats also protected cowboys from thorns and low-hanging branches. Cowboys even used them to carry water, to fan or put out fires, and as pillows.

The cowboys' other clothing was also practical. Their shirts and pants were made of strong material. They lasted a long time and protected the cowboys' skin. When it was dusty, cowboys covered their noses and mouths with the bandannas they wore around their necks.

When riding horses, cowboys used their boot heels to prevent their feet from slipping out of the stirrups. When roping cattle, the cowboys could dig their boot heels into the ground.

UNIT 6

How do we know what is true?

UNIT TEST

LISTENING AND READING COMPREHENSION

DIRECTIONS

Listen to the passage "Oh, Brother!" Then choose the best answer for each item. Circle the letter for the correct answer.

1. Gerry likes to tell _____.
   A. stories
   B. lies
   C. riddles
   D. secrets

2. Who is telling the story?
   A. Gerry's younger brother
   B. Gerry's older brother
   C. Gerry's favorite uncle
   D. Gerry's best friend

3. Most of the story takes place _____.
   A. in Gerry's bedroom
   B. in the basement
   C. at the library
   D. in the kitchen

4. How does the narrator change by the end of the story?
   A. He feels hungry.
   B. He is nicer to Gerry.
   C. He is smart and cool.
   D. He tells his own riddles.

DIRECTIONS

Read the questions about the readings "How Glooskap Found the Summer" and "Persephone an the Pomegranate Seeds". Choose the best answer for each item. Circle the letter of the correct answer.

"How Glooskap Found the Summer"

5. Why does Glooskap travel north to visit Winter?
   A. He visits Winter because he likes cold weather.
   B. He visits Winter because his people need help.
   C. He visits Winter because Summer is too hot.
   D. He visits Winter because his father tells him to.

6. Summer helps Glooskap by _____.
   A. overpowering Winter
   B. buying him warm winter clothing
   C. running home to her land in the south
   D. waking Glooskap from his magical sleep

"Persephone and the Pomegranate Seeds"

7. Pluto gives Persephone _____.
   A. twelve beautiful flowers
   B. twelve pomegranate seeds
   C. many trees and plants on earth
   D. a fine chariot and two matching horses

8. Why did Pluto give them to Persephone?
   A. He thought she would become a beautiful flower.
   B. He wanted her to stay with him in the underworld.
   C. He wanted her to plant a garden in the underworld.
   D. He was ordered to by Zeus, the king of the gods.

DIRECTIONS

Read the questions about the reading "Early Astronomers." Choose the best answer for each item. Circle the letter of the correct answer.

9. How was a calendar useful to people long ago?
   A. It showed people when to plant and when to harvest.
   B. It showed people when to celebrate birthdays and festivals.
   C. It showed people when to take vacations to foreign lands.
   D. It showed people how to spell the months of the year.

10. The Persian astronomer who identified more than 1,000 stars was _____.
    A. Copernicus
    B. Aristotle
    C. Al-Sufi
    D. Kepler

11. Nicholas Copernicus is considered the founder of modern astronomy because _____.
    A. he supported his theories with complex calculations
    B. he believed the sun was the center of the solar system
    C. he developed a powerful telescope that is still used today
    D. he discovered the orbits of the planets around the sun are oval-shaped

12. "The father of modern science" is _____.
    A. Al-Sufi
    B. Galileo
    C. Kelper
    D. Copernicus

Name _____ Date _____

DIRECTIONS

Read the questions about the reading selection from *The War of the Worlds*. Choose the best answer for each item. Circle the letter of the correct answer.

13. At the beginning of the broadcast, what does Professor Pierson think the object is?
    A. a spaceship
    B. a big joke
    C. a meteorite
    D. a tornado

14. The object really is _____.
    A. a meteorite
    B. an alien
    C. a ball of glowing fire
    D. an explosion from underground

15. The crowd begins to move away from the object because _____.
    A. Carl Phillips orders them to
    B. the object frightens them
    C. the people are bored and tired
    D. Mr. Wilmuth calls the police

16. What happens at the end of the play?
    A. Everyone left on the scene is arrested.
    B. The field is set on fire and people die.
    C. Carl Phillips climbs into the pit.
    D. The object vanishes in a puff of smoke.

DIRECTIONS

Read the questions about the reading "Earth's Orbit." Choose the best answer for each item. Circle the letter of the correct answer.

17. Why do the sun and moon seem to move across the sky each day?
    A. They seem to move because they are revolving around the earth.
    B. They seem to move because the Earth is turning on its axis.
    C. They seem to move because the Earth orbits the sun each day.
    D. They seem to move because the wind pushes them to the west.

18. Earth goes around the sun in _____.
    A. 6 hours
    B. 24 hours
    C. 48 hours
    D. 365 days

19. When is it summer in the Northern Hemisphere?
    A. It is summer in June, July, and August.
    B. It is summer in September, October, and November.
    C. It is summer in December, January, and February.
    D. It is summer in March, April, and May.

20. When the noon sun is directly overhead at the equator there is a(n) _____.
    A. equinox
    B. solstice
    C. synapse
    D. rotation

VOCABULARY

DIRECTIONS

Choose the word or words that best complete each sentence. Circle the letter of the correct answer.

21. Particular groups of stars named after something they seem to picture in an outline are called _____.
    A. conjugations
    B. discoveries
    C. syncopations
    D. constellations

22. A tube-shaped device used to make faraway objects look bigger and closer is a _____.
    A. galaxy
    B. telescope
    C. solar system
    D. phenomenon

23. Two times a year, night and day have equal lengths. This is called a(n) _____.
    A. solstice
    B. equinox
    C. equator
    D. estuary

24. When something turns in a circular motion around a central point, it is known as _____.
    A. osmosis
    B. rotation
    C. navigation
    D. denotation

25. A fictional story passed down through the generations to explain natural events such as wind and rain is called a _____.
    A. myth
    B. quote
    C. sign
    D. twig

26. *Everyone tried to help, but it was Sara who saved her little brother.* Sara is the story's _____.
    A. myth
    B. villain
    C. heron
    D. heroine

27. A type of literature with imaginary events that involve science and technology is called _____.
    A. technical writing
    B. creative nonfiction
    C. science fiction
    D. historical fiction

28. *Anil walks arcoss the room and looks out the window. "It's snowing!" he shouts.* This is an example of _____.
    A. dramatic flair
    B. stage directions
    C. actors' directives
    D. authors' commands

Name _____ Date _____

DIRECTIONS
Choose the word or words that best complete each sentence. Circle the letter of the correct answer.

29. To make something as good as it was before is to _____.
    A. respond
    B. repeat
    C. restore
    D. review

30. Something usual, expected, or obvious is _____.
    A. predictable
    B. marvelous
    C. accidental
    D. edible

31. A slightly changed copy of something is a _____.
    A. role
    B. version
    C. location
    D. philosopher

32. A solid round shape like a ball is a _____.
    A. cloister
    B. sphere
    C. sonnet
    D. phase

GO ON

WORD STUDY

DIRECTIONS

Read each question below and find the correct answer. Circle the letter of the correct word.

33. What is the antonym of *found*?
    A. find
    B. lost
    C. took
    D. stayed

34. What is the antonym of *winter*?
    A. autumn
    B. spring
    C. summer
    D. foliage

35. What is the antonym of *weak*?
    A. thin
    B. strong
    C. friendly
    D. sad

36. Which word has a long *i* sound?
    A. crisp
    B. swim
    C. miss
    D. flight

37. Which word has a short *i* sound?
    A. life
    B. fly
    C. drip
    D. pie

38. Which word has a long *i* sound?
    A. shrimp
    B. price
    C. whisk
    D. dinner

DIRECTIONS

Read each question below and find the correct answer. Circle the letter of the correct answer.

39. Which word has the correct ending?
    A. sensible
    B. describible
    C. suitible
    D. laughible

40. Which word has the correct ending?
    A. horrable
    B. possable
    C. available
    D. incredable

41. Which word has the correct ending?
    A. habitible
    B. terrible
    C. comfortible
    D. suitible

42. Which word root means "turn"?
    A. *rev-*
    B. *geo-*
    C. *equ-*
    D. *cycl-*

43. Which word root means "earth"?
    A. *astro-*
    B. *kilo-*
    C. *geo-*
    D. *equ-*

44. Which word root means "circle, ring"?
    A. *rota-*
    B. *astro-*
    C. *kilo-*
    D. *cycl-*

GRAMMAR

DIRECTIONS
Choose the word or words that best complete each sentence. Circle the letter of the correct answer.

45. We _____ paint the garage. It took a week, but we finished!
A. have to
B. had to
C. can
D. must

46. Usha and Juan were _____ to win a prize at the science fair.
A. excited
B. exciting
C. disappointed
D. disappointing

47. The movie was _____.
A. bored
B. boring
C. going
D. ended

48. *"You are all invited to my birthday party, Victor announced.* In the above sentence, quotation marks are needed _____.
A. after *party,* after the comma
B. after *party,* before the comma
C. after *announced,* before the period
D. after *announced,* after the period

49. Jamal is kind and generous. Therefore, _____.
A. he is good in sports
B. he has a mean sister
C. he has many friends
D. he never gets sick

50. _____, so people are driving slowly.
A. It is warm
B. It is Friday
C. It is icy
D. It is cool

51. We _____ recycle to help the planet!
A. must
B. couldn't
C. may
D. haven't

52. The view from the Grand Canyon is _____.
A. being amazed
B. amaze
C. amazed
D. amazing

53. *Dr. Chin said, Where does it hurt?"* In the above sentence, quotation marks are needed _____.
A. before *Dr.*
B. between *Chin* and *said*
C. after *said,* before the comma
D. after the comma, before *Where*

54. *"Tomorrow is the field trip, the teacher said.* In the above sentence, quotation marks are needed _____.
A. after *trip,* before the comma
B. after *trip,* after the comma
C. after *said,* before the period
D. after *said,* after the period

55. The sun is shining brightly. As a result, _____.
A. the ice is melting fast
B. it will snow again today
C. people are staying inside
D. it will be cold tonight

GO ON

THE BIG QUESTION

How do we know what is true?

DIRECTIONS

Explain what kind of research you could do to find out whether something you have heard or read about is true or not. Write on the lines below.

_____

_____

_____

_____

_____

_____

_____

_____

_____

_____

_____

_____

_____

_____

_____

_____

_____

_____

_____

ORAL READING FLUENCY SCORE SHEET

Galileo, the Italian physicist, mathematician, astronomer, and	7
philosopher, is often called the father of modern science. He asked	18
questions, made observations, and tested his theories. This would later	28
be known as "the scientific method" of investigation.	36

In 1609, Galileo learned about the invention of the telescope. 46

He improved the design of the telescope so that it gave a much better 60

view of the stars and planets. His telescope magnified objects to thirty 72

times their real size. He discovered that the Milky Way is made up of 86

millions of stars. He also discovered Saturn's rings and Jupiter's 96

moons. Amazingly, no additional moons of Jupiter were discovered 105

until 400 years later, in 2002. 111

Galileo believed that earth traveled around the sun. He 120

published his theories and findings in the book *Dialogue on the Two* 132

Great World Systems. Galileo was warned by the Roman Catholic 142

Church to stop teaching his theories, but Galileo refused. He was 153

brought before the Inquisition, a religious court. The court found him 164

guilty of speaking against the Church's beliefs.

Fluency Skill Assessed	Points Possible	Points Earned
Student reads with speed.	2	
Student reads with accuracy.	2	
Student reads with expression.	2	
Student reads with intonation.	2	
Student self-corrects.	2	

Total Score _____ / 10

Unit 6 • Unit Test Oral Reading Fluency   **191**

DIRECTIONS
Read the text below aloud for your teacher. Read with speed, accuracy, expression, and intonation.

Galileo, the Italian physicist, mathematician, astronomer, and philosopher, is often called the father of modern science. He asked questions, made observations, and tested his theories. This would later be known as "the scientific method" of investigation.

In 1609, Galileo learned about the invention of the telescope. He improved the design of the telescope so that it gave a much better view of the stars and planets. His telescope magnified objects to thirty times their real size. He discovered that the Milky Way is made up of millions of stars. He also discovered Saturn's rings and Jupiter's moons. Amazingly, no additional moons of Jupiter were discovered until 400 years later, in 2002.

Galileo believed that Earth traveled around the sun. He published his theories and findings in the book *Dialogue on the Two Great World Systems*. Galileo was warned by the Roman Catholic Church to stop teaching his theories, but Galileo refused. He was brought before the Inquisition, a religious court. The court found him guilty of speaking against the Church's beliefs.

TEST PREPARATION

Taking a Test
Strategy: Understand Directions Before You Take a Test

Most tests have directions that tell you what to do. Sometimes your teacher will read the directions to you. Other times you will read them yourself. Listen or read carefully. Be sure you understand the directions before you begin the test.

> Understanding directions before you take the test will help you
> • know what to do on a test.
> • answer questions correctly.

Practice this strategy by answering the questions on the next page. Follow these steps:

1. Listen to or read the directions carefully.
2. Look for important words in the directions.
3. If you don't understand a word, use context clues to help you figure out the meaning of the word. Context clues are the words that come before and after the word you don't know.
4. Raise your hand and ask for help if you don't understand the directions.
5. Follow the directions to answer each question.
6. Sometimes there is more than one set of directions on a page. Repeat steps 1–5 above each time you see new directions.
7. Look for directions at the bottom of the page.

   If you see **GO ON**, it means you should go on to answer the questions on the next page.

   If you see **STOP**, do not go on to the next page. If you finish a test early, go back and check your answers.

Name _____ Date _____

DIRECTIONS
Choose the word or words that best complete each sentence. Circle the letter of the correct answer.

1. A cat's babies are called _____.
   A. cubs
   B. puppies
   C. ducklings
   D. kittens

2. The season after spring is _____.
   A. winter
   B. fall
   C. summer
   D. July

DIRECTIONS
Choose the correct word for each definition below. Circle the letter of the correct answer.

3. _____: someone who teaches
   A. instructor
   B. sculptor
   C. inventor
   D. conductor

4. _____: very; more than usual
   A. less
   B. especially
   C. partly
   D. probably

DIRECTIONS
Read each sentence below. Circle the letter of the underlined word that is spelled incorrectly.

5. A. I have two cats and three <u>dogs</u>.
   B. They have two <u>boyes</u>.
   C. There are many <u>bridges</u>.
   D. New York and Atlanta are <u>cities</u>.

6. A. I read about twenty <u>pages</u>.
   B. He needs new <u>shoes</u>.
   C. Those are cute <u>babys</u>.
   D. <u>Bears</u> live in forests.

DIRECTIONS
Read each question below. Circle the letter of the correct word or words.

7. Which word has a short *i* sound?
   A. cry
   B. high
   C. try
   D. miss

8. Which word has a long *i* sound?
   A. list
   B. hit
   C. right
   D. kiss

STOP

Test Preparation • Taking a Test

Answering Questions about a Passage
Strategy: Preview the Title, Passage, and Questions

Some tests have passages such as short stories, poems, or history or science texts. The tests also have items that ask about the passages. Before you read each passage, preview the title, the passage, and the questions. When you preview, you look at the title, the passage, and the questions to find out what the passage is about and what the questions ask.

Previewing the title, the passage, and the questions will help you
- decide how to read the passage.
- think about what you will need to know to answer the questions.

Practice this strategy by answering the questions on the next page. Follow these steps:

1. Look at the title and the first sentence in each paragraph in the passage. Ask yourself, "Is this passage fiction or nonfiction? What is this passage mostly about?"

2. Then decide how to read the passage. If the passage is nonfiction, or if it tells about something you don't know much about, you should read the passage slowly and carefully. If the passage is fiction, or if it tells about something you already know, you can probably read the passage more quickly.

3. Look at any art that goes with the passage, such as a picture, a chart, or a map. Ask yourself, "What does the art tell me about the passage?"

4. Look at the questions. Find out what information you need to know to answer the questions. For example, find out if you need to know about the main idea or a character's feelings. Then look for this information as you read the passage.

5. Read the passage. Don't worry if you do not understand all the words. You need to understand enough information to answer the questions.

6. Follow the directions to answer each question. Look back at the passage as often as you like to help you answer the questions. You don't have to reread the whole passage. Look for information that helps you answer the questions. If you are allowed to write in your test, underline key words that help you answer the questions.

7. Don't spend too much time on a question. If you can't decide what the best answer is, circle the number of the question. If you have time at the end of the test, you can go back and finish any questions you circled.

DIRECTIONS
Read the passage. Then choose the best answer for each item. Circle the letter of the correct answer.

Frieda's Special Birthday Present

Frieda told her parents that she wanted a puppy for her birthday. Her parents weren't sure if they should give Frieda a puppy. They didn't know if Frieda could take care of a young pet. Dad told Frieda, "A puppy is a lot of work. You have to walk it and feed it every day."

Frieda said, "I can take good care of a puppy. I know I can do a good job!"

On her birthday, Frieda got some nice presents, but she didn't get a puppy. Then Mom said, "Wait a minute. Your father has one more present for you." Frieda heard barking! Dad came into the room and put a small, brown puppy on the floor.

"Happy Birthday!" her parents said. Frieda smiled as the puppy licked her hand. She loved the puppy, and she was glad that her parents believed she could take care of it.

---

1. This passage is _____.
   A. a play
   B. fiction
   C. a poem
   D. a history text

2. You can tell from the title that this passage is about _____.
   A. taking care of a puppy
   B. making a birthday present
   C. the day Frieda was born
   D. a birthday present for Frieda

3. Why weren't Frieda's parents sure they should give Frieda a puppy?
   A. They did not want to have a pet.
   B. Frieda does not like dogs.
   C. They thought the puppy would make a big mess.
   D. They did not know if Frieda could take care of a puppy.

4. How does Frieda feel at the end?
   A. nervous
   B. happy
   C. upset
   D. tired

STOP

Answering Multiple-Choice Questions
Strategy: Read, Think, Look, and Choose

A multiple-choice question has three or four answer choices, but only one choice is the correct answer. You have to choose the best answer for each question. To answer a multiple-choice question, remember to *read* the question, *think* about the correct answer, *look* at all the answer choices, and then *choose* the best answer.

Reading, thinking, looking, and choosing will help you
- use your own knowledge to answer the question.
- choose the best answer for the question.

Practice this strategy by answering the questions on the next page. Follow these steps:

1. Read the question.
2. Cover up the answer choices with your hand.
3. Think of the correct answer.
4. After you have an idea of the correct answer, move your hand and look at the answer choices. Read each choice. Find the answer choice that is closest to your answer. This choice should be the best answer.
5. If the question asks about a passage and you are not sure of the answer, look back at the passage to try to find information that answers the question.
6. Don't spend too much time on a question. If you can't decide what the best answer is, circle the number of the question. You can come back to answer this question later if you have time.
7. When you finish answering all the questions, check your answers. If you have carefully thought about all the answer choices for a question, then the first answer you chose is the one most likely to be correct.

DIRECTIONS

Read the passage. Then choose the best answer for each item. Circle the letter of the correct answer.

How Armadillo Got His Shell

Long ago, Armadillo was a furry animal. One day, he chased Spider. Spider crawled under a bush with sharp thorns. Spider knew that Armadillo would not go under the bush because the sharp thorns would scratch Armadillo's furry skin. Armadillo waited for Spider to come out. He began to get hungry. Armadillo stretched his tongue as far as it would go, but it was not long enough to reach Spider.

Then Turtle passed under the bush.

"Don't the thorns scratch you?" Armadillo asked.

"Oh, no," Turtle replied. "My shell is very thick. The thorns can't scratch me."

"Where can I find a thick shell like yours?" Armadillo asked.

Turtle told Armadillo, "Wait for some rain and roll in the mud. Then lie in the hot sun. The sun will turn the mud into a thick shell."

So Armadillo followed Turtle's directions. To this day, all armadillos have thick shells to protect them wherever they go.

---

1. What problem does Armadillo have in this passage?
   A. He is afraid of Spider.
   B. He is tired from chasing Spider.
   C. He can't reach Spider under the thorn bush.
   D. Turtle will not let Armadillo get near Spider.

2. Spider crawled under the bush with thorns because _____.
   A. it was cool under the bush
   B. he thought Armadillo would stay away
   C. he wanted to be near his friend Turtle
   D. he thought Armadillo couldn't see him

3. Turtle doesn't get scratched by the thorns because _____.
   A. he moves slowly
   B. he is not very big
   C. his thick shell protects him
   D. he digs under the bush

4. How does Armadillo change by the end of the story?
   A. He doesn't chase Spider anymore.
   B. He stays away from bushes with thorns.
   C. He and Turtle become best friends.
   D. He gets a hard shell that protects him.

STOP

Answering Questions about Meanings of Words
Strategy: Use Context Clues

Some tests have questions that ask about the meanings of words. Use context clues to help you figure out the meaning of a word that is unfamiliar to you. Context clues are the words before and after the word you don't know. They help explain the meaning of the word.

> Using context clues will help you
> - figure out the meaning of a word you don't know.
> - choose the best answer for a question about the meaning of a word.

Practice this strategy by answering the questions on the next page. Follow these steps:

1. Read the question. Find the word the question asks about. This word is sometimes a word that you don't know.
2. Skim the passage quickly to find the word the question asks about.
3. Look at the words before and after the word that you don't know. Look for clues that help explain the meaning of the word.
4. Read the answer choices. Find the answer choice that gives the best meaning of the word.
5. Some questions ask you to find another word that means the *same* as the word in the question. For these questions, follow steps 1–3 above. Then compare the word in the question to the words in the answer choices. Find the word in the answer choices that has a meaning that is the same or almost the same as the word in the question. For example, *big* and *large* have the same meanings.
6. Some questions ask you to find the word that means the *opposite* of the word in the question. For these questions, follow steps 1–3 above. Then think about the meaning of each of the answer choices. The answer choice that has the meaning that is the most different from the meaning of the word in the question is the best answer. For example, *unhappy* is the opposite of *happy*, and *up* is the opposite of *down*.

DIRECTIONS
Read the passage. Then choose the best answer for each item. Circle the letter of the correct answer.

The Water Cycle

Most of Earth is covered with water. The amount of water on Earth never changes, but the water often changes from one form to another. For example, the water in the ocean is one <u>form</u>, or kind, of water.

The water cycle is the way that Earth's water changes its form and moves. A <u>cycle</u> is a series of things that happens over and over again in the same order. Earth's water moves from the oceans up into the air. Then it moves from the air down to the land and back into the oceans.

The sun's heat makes some of Earth's water <u>evaporate</u>. The water turns to water vapor, a gas that you can't see. The water vapor <u>rises</u> in the air. When the water vapor cools, it becomes rain, snow, sleet, or hail and falls to the land. The rain runs into lakes, rivers, and oceans. The sun's heat melts some snow and ice back to water. This water also runs into lakes, rivers, and oceans. Then the water cycle starts all over again.

1. What does the word <u>cycle</u> mean in this passage?
   A. something that happens once
   B. something that turns into a gas
   C. something that you do on a bicycle
   D. something that repeats again and again

2. When water <u>evaporates</u>, it becomes _____.
   A. rain
   B. snow
   C. a gas
   D. a river

3. In this passage, the word <u>form</u> means the same as _____.
   A. ice
   B. many
   C. kind
   D. amount

4. Which word is the opposite of the word <u>rises</u>?
   A. falls
   B. lifts
   C. floats
   D. light

STOP

Answering Fill-in-the-Blank Items
Strategy: Try Every Answer Choice

Some tests have items that give you a sentence with a word missing. You have to find the word that best completes the sentence. For these items, try every answer choice to find the word that fits best in the sentence.

Trying every answer choice will help you
- think about the answer choices.
- choose the best answer for a fill-in-the-blank item.

Practice this strategy by answering the items on the next page. Follow these steps:

1. Read the item or the sentence with a missing word.
2. Look at the first answer choice. Fill in the blank in the sentence with this word. Reread the sentence with the first answer choice in the blank.
3. Ask yourself, "Does the sentence make sense with this answer choice? Does this answer choice complete the sentence correctly?"
4. Repeat steps 2 and 3 for each of the other answer choices. Find the word that best completes the sentence with a blank in it.
5. If you can write in your test, you may want to write the answer choices above the blank in the sentence so you can read the complete sentence.
6. Don't spend too much time on an item. If you can't decide what the best answer is, circle the number of the item. If you have time at the end of the test, you can go back and finish any items you circled.

GO ON

DIRECTIONS
Read each pair of sentences. Look at the underlined word or words in the first sentence. Then choose the correct pronoun to complete the second sentence. Circle the letter of the correct answer.

1. <u>Han and Ed</u> play soccer. _____ are the best players on the team.
   A. They
   B. Him
   C. He
   D. It

2. The girl feeds her two <u>dogs</u>. She gives _____ food in the morning and at night.
   A. her
   B. it
   C. them
   D. us

DIRECTIONS
Choose the word that best completes each sentence. Circle the letter of the correct answer.

3. Sam _____ Lila ride to the park together.
   A. or
   B. and
   C. but
   D. with

4. During quiet time, students can either read books _____ draw pictures.
   A. or
   B. and
   C. but
   D. with

5. The _____ sun melted the ice.
   A. hot
   B. are
   C. and
   D. snow

6. Now we _____ in a blue house.
   A. live
   B. lives
   C. lived
   D. living

STOP

Responding to a Writing Prompt
Strategy: Think, Plan, Write, and Check

Some tests ask you to write about a topic. A writing test has a writing prompt with directions that tell you what to write about. When you take a writing test, *think* about the topic, *plan* what you will write about, *write* your response, and then *check* your writing.

Thinking, planning, writing, and checking will help you
- use your time well during a writing test.
- write a good response.

Practice this strategy by looking at the directions on the next page and writing a response. Follow these steps:

1. Read the directions in the writing prompt. The directions tell what you should write about. Be sure you understand the directions.
2. Think about the topic. The topic is the subject or idea that the directions ask you to write about. Sometimes you can use your own experiences to help you decide what you will write.
3. Plan your writing. Sometimes your teacher will give you extra paper for planning. At other times there will be space in the test for planning. Write notes to plan what you will write about. Use a word web, a list, a chart, or an outline to help you organize your ideas.
4. Write about the topic. Be sure you do everything that the directions ask you to do.
5. When you write a short story, it should have a beginning, middle, and end. Expository writing should have a main idea and supporting details. When you describe something, use adjectives that are clear and interesting. When you explain how to do something, list steps in the right order. When you try to persuade readers to do something or ask them to agree with your opinion, give good reasons that explain your ideas.
6. When you finish writing, check your work. Be sure all your sentences are complete and all words are spelled correctly.
7. Don't spend too much time on any step when writing. Find out how much time you have for the writing test. Spend some time thinking about the topic. Spend most of your time planning and writing. Be sure to leave enough time to check your writing.

WRITING PROMPT

Think of an interesting gift that someone gave to you or that you gave to someone. Write a descriptive paragraph about this gift. Tell what the gift is and why you think it is interesting. Be sure to include details in your writing. Write on the lines below.

STOP

Test Preparation • Responding to a Writing Prompt